Mending My Mind

Mending My Mind

Sara Church

Mending My Mind
© 2021 Sara Church

This book is a memoir. It reflects the author's present recollections of experiences over time. Names and identifiable characteristics or details of characters have been changed to protect their privacy.

Published by Pyrus Publishing
pyruspublishing.com

Paperback ISBN: 979-8-9850357-0-4
Hardcover ISBN: 979-8-9850357-2-8
Ebook ISBN: 979-8-9850357-1-1
Audiobook ISBN: 979-8-9850357-3-5

Cover design by Emily Mahon
Interior design by Liz Schreiter
Edited and produced by Reading List Editorial
ReadingListEditorial.com

Per aspera ad astra
Through adversity to the stars

Disclaimer

This book deals with topics including childhood trauma, homicide, relational problems, and fertility that may be troubling for some readers. The author has been careful to ensure the subject matter is dealt with in a respectful manner, without sensationalizing it or dramatizing it, and has changed details and information about key characters to protect their identities and their private information.

The content of this book is not intended to diagnose, treat, cure, or prevent any mental health condition, and it is not a substitute for consultation with a licensed mental health practitioner.

Preface

When I turned forty, my life seemed great. I was married to a terrific woman, I had a successful career in biotech doing meaningful work, and I enjoyed my friendships. On the surface, my life was peaceful, and I was content.

Yet, I was unfulfilled and a workaholic. My wife and I had grown apart so much that divorce was on the table.

Of course, this happens to couples all the time and people are able to move through it. But I couldn't. I went into a tailspin, uncovering long-buried skeletons from my past. My days became filled with numbness, anxiety, and shame; my nights with fear and nightmares. At times, the world started to seem unreal, as if I were watching a movie.

I didn't understand why I felt so profoundly troubled, and I couldn't explain what was happening. What I did know—once I discovered I had trauma-induced amnesia—was that I couldn't avoid dealing with it by pretending that I had it all together.

To seek answers, I sought therapy. In fact, I saw six therapists over the course of three years. I discovered that, unbeknownst to me, I had complex post-traumatic stress disorder (c-PTSD). Beneath the veneer of my generally calm exterior lay a history of childhood trauma, some of which I couldn't even remember, and all of which was unresolved. This prevented me from connecting with my wife and from connecting to myself and knowing my essence. Until my past was brought to the surface and healed, I would remain deeply unsettled and disconnected. The worst part was I hurt people I loved because of my inability to tolerate or sustain intimate relationships.

My story is far too common. According to the CDC, 61 percent of people have had at least one adverse childhood experience, which is a potentially traumatic event that can change brain development, affect how the body responds to stress, and create difficulty in relationships.[1] Unresolved trauma can also wound others—including our kids, when we pass it along to them—if it's left untreated. Even though my PTSD was not my fault, it was my responsibility to address it.

But dealing with my past was a gut-wrenching slog. In order to change my life, I had to mend my mind. I had to untangle the damage that was done to my nervous system and rewire my brain. I stuck with it, determined to live a more meaningful life, one with closer relationships with my family and friends. And I also wanted to become a parent. So, I did the work. I fell—a ton—and I got up and kept plugging away. While life didn't necessarily become easy, it did become a whole lot better.

This book began as a journal. Writing was one of the techniques I used to heal. I got involved with the CPTSD Foundation, where the stories this community courageously shared helped me. Later, I found the guts to publish an essay, and that experience empowered me to come forward about my PTSD. More people speaking up and sharing their stories about mental health, I believe, will help others. Since the pandemic started, I've been inspired by the increase in public conversation around this topic, and I'm optimistic that the discussion is a step in the right direction toward better health and well-being as well as access to mental health resources. And maybe if we heal ourselves, we will be better able to improve our world.

Trauma-related disorders are often underdiagnosed, undertreated, mistreated, and minimized. If you or someone you love is suffering, I am sorry.

Healing is possible. Here is my human story.

---

1 Centers for Disease Control, "Preventing Adverse Childhood Experiences," page last reviewed 2021, cdc.gov/violenceprevention/aces/fastfact.html.

PART I

I have come to the conclusion that human beings are born with an innate capacity to triumph over trauma. I believe not only that trauma is curable, but that the healing process can be a catalyst for profound awakening—a portal opening to emotional and genuine spiritual transformation.
—Dr. Peter Levine

1

On an uncharacteristically bright January day in 2018, I sat on my deck staring at the majestic mountains that flank Seattle.

The weather was sunny. But, inside, a perfect storm gathered.

"Sara! Would you like a cappuccino?" my wife, Elizabeth, called.

My mind went blank. I wasn't sure how to answer my wonderful Elizabeth, the woman I loved but who I was contemplating leaving. As I held back my tears, I thought about her many kind gestures, like bringing me coffee.

"No thanks," I replied, feeling the weight of my heart in my chest. Elizabeth, who had striking dark eyes and bronze skin, was beautiful inside and out. More importantly, she was a loyal, smart, and loving person. A person who supportively said yes when I asked her if we could adopt a dog. The one who made sure we brought a bottle of wine or a gift when we went over to a friend's house.

Elizabeth, being pragmatic, brought balance to my various ideas. "They are signing up volunteers for the Mars colony," I said one day, after reading an article on the topic. I imagined the great adventure that would be living on another planet. And I pictured us watering plants in the martian soil next to our rover.

"That is too far away from my family," she said, nudging me back into reality. We balanced each other out.

Elizabeth and I met through mutual friends. Our group was diverse, though we all worked for the same biotech company in Los Angeles: we had friends from different countries with various life experiences.

At work, each day was a new experience, one that oozed with excitement and ideas. We were relatively young and energetic. We all shared a love of science and an enjoyment of good food, fascinating talks, game nights, and weekend trips to explore California's wonders. We worked hard and we had fun together outside of work.

Everything changed one evening when Elizabeth walked into one of our happy hours. She caught my attention right away. She was a classy woman wearing a silk scarf around her neck and carrying a *New Yorker* in her purse. I introduced myself to her, my white hands trembling during our handshake, and awkwardly took a seat next to her. As our table buzzed with conversation, I proceeded by not saying a word—that is, until the topic of scuba diving came up. Then, quietly, I mentioned to the group, "It's like traveling to another world. A beautiful one. Diving is one of my favorite things to do."

"Mine, too," said Elizabeth. I felt a magnetic pull toward her, and we became good friends.

Our relationship evolved the night that she brought her homemade guacamole to my roommate Raj's dinner party. After polishing off a couple of margaritas, I walked into my bedroom and found Elizabeth sitting on my bed. She peered at me, and a chill ran down my spine. I sensed that this was a turning point.

I was but I also wasn't surprised by this progression. There had been subtle cues and some nervous flirtation. The side glances, the lingering smiles, and our bodies mirroring each other when we chatted were early signs of us falling in love. I woke up the next morning spooning her, the two of us still wearing our clothes from the night before.

Within weeks, we were a couple. And a year and a half later, we got married in a Malibu vineyard by a Black female priest who gazed at us with reassuring brown eyes. It was 2014, almost a year before same-sex marriage was legal in all fifty states. The ceremony was attended by our family and our closest friends. Elizabeth wore a long floral dress and I wore a leprechaun-green dress. I looked like the leaf to her flower.

Both independent people, we kept our own last names and bank accounts.

We both traveled regularly for work, and for several months, I would fly out of LA on a Monday morning, on Virgin Airlines with neon lights, hip music floating through the air, and return back to LA that Thursday. I wasn't sure if this life fit me, but it was cool. We missed each other, but we enjoyed flying into each other's arms after several days apart.

However, if she seemed preoccupied when I walked through the door—for instance, one time she was on the phone and only waved at me—I would feel crushed, worried she was losing interest. But then I would brush it off.

A couple of years after we were married, I was ready to take a risk. I wanted to be part of a start-up in Seattle that was working on a new approach to treat cancer: a cell therapy with the potential to be a game-changing treatment for cancer patients. "I'll sweep the floors," I practically begged my boss during my interview. And I came home and pleaded my case to Elizabeth. "This opportunity is special. I believe cell and gene therapy could cure cancer one day. And other diseases too. Plus the people at the company are amazing."

It would be a sacrifice for Elizabeth. She had a successful job in biotech, and we loved life in LA. And yet she wished to be supportive, and she believed in the cause of the start-up, too. So, just two years into our marriage, we moved from sunny Los Angeles to rainy Seattle.

We bought an uber-modern three-bedroom house with concrete floors and large glass windows. And we took advantage of the many things the Pacific Northwest has to offer, like seeing the San Juan Islands, skiing in Whistler, eating great seafood, and visiting museums.

Weekend mornings were our favorite. We woke up leisurely and cuddled, we drank coffee and read the *New York Times*, and we took our beagle, Leo, on a walk along Lake Union.

Life was peaceful. Life was easy. And our marriage was good.

Yet something had been going off course, and I had missed the signs. Although I loved Elizabeth, we didn't share ourselves at the deepest levels. We swept our conflicts under the rug, and we didn't talk about our hopes or our dreams for our future.

And now, after five years together, our spark was gone. Most nights, we got into bed, we said goodnight and, after we kissed each other on the cheek, we turned to our respective sides of the bed.

The change in our relationship was low key—there was no yelling and no drama. We went from laughing together to avoiding each other and living separate lives. I was a workaholic. I checked my emails as we ate dinner and then I would retreat to do more work until bedtime. Elizabeth would watch TV or go out with friends, and she would look forward to her regular business trips to New York. We were both in our clamshells, and neither of us wanted to approach this change in our relationship.

I blamed myself for the disconnection in our relationship. Was I even capable of love? I had a history of running away from intimacy and ending relationships. And while I took our vows—"for better or for worse"—seriously and had all intentions of staying married to Elizabeth until the day I died, a part of me wanted to bolt. I recalled how, years ago, when I asked Elizabeth to marry me, I accidentally dropped the engagement ring on the ground. Sigmund Freud could have made much of that. *What lurked beneath the surface that kept me from true intimacy? What was wrong with me?*

Deep down, I sensed I was troubled, but I buried those nudges. And for a long time, avoidance worked—until it didn't. Throughout my life, I had experienced extreme tension and emotional numbness when confronted with the risk of loss or rejection, but I always shoved those feelings down. During times of extreme duress, I would detach myself and watch my life as if it were a movie, all the while acting normal. And in this movie, I was the character who was contemplating walking out on her marriage.

I thought that Elizabeth would be lucky to have me out of her life. I wouldn't have touched a partner as difficult as me with a ten-foot pole.

2

Hugo House, a creative space for local writers, sits in Seattle's edgy Capitol Hill neighborhood. A historic-looking house, where the rooms are filled with comfy chairs around wooden tables, it invites writers from all walks of life to take classes, debate, and collaborate. Thermoses of coffee and Hydro Flasks are omnipresent, as is the almond odor of old books.

One day, I decided to take the leap and enroll in their "Philosophy for Poets" course, since no experience in philosophy was required.

Throughout my life, poems have occasionally and randomly spilled from my pen as if someone else was guiding my hand. This always startled me, and I would wad up and toss the poems after I wrote them. The creative vibe of Seattle encouraged me to finally explore my hidden interest in poetry.

The course argued that philosophy and poetry come from the same source—thinking—but my poems came from an unknown feeling source from inside me. The only common point, the class agreed on, between poetry and philosophy is that they both involve words. To demonstrate how poets show thinking, the course looked at philosophical poems by Rilke, Goethe, and Ryan. We had exploratory in-class writing, as well as reading assignments for homework. I carried Plato's *The Republic* in my work bag for a month, leafing through it as I ate my lunch.

Dressed in my usual corporate outfit—high heels, a blazer with a V-neck tee underneath, and designer jeans—I looked like I had just left a business meeting, which I had. This created an immediate feeling of insecurity on my first day of class. Would they think I was too left-brained to fit in? Thankfully, I was wearing my thick, black eyeglasses. My classmates—a Black professor with a tweed jacket, a middle-aged white woman wearing a beanie and a flannel, an Indian woman with a tattooed arm sleeve, a pale bald man with round, clear-plastic glasses and a black button-up shirt—all had that quintessential writer look.

I plopped down next to a fascinating-looking woman. She had a brown pixie haircut, hazel eyes, porcelain skin, and a loose blouse that had abstract elephants on it, an organic Pacific Northwest look. Her blouse especially had an effect on me, and I immediately respected her persona, which stated "I'm an individual, I love animals, and I don't care what people think of me."

She smiled warmly at me and introduced herself as Claire. I later learned that she was a published author who was thriving in her field. This intimidated me a bit and added to my self-doubt.

I was immediately struck by her unique appearance and confidence. My heart thumped away as I nervously kneaded my shirt. While looking away, I mumbled, "I'm Sara. Nice to meet you."

The class read from the works of Plato. When my turn came, I read a line from *The Republic* that struck me: "But tell me, this physician of whom you were just speaking, is he a moneymaker, an earner of fees, or a healer of the sick?"

When class ended, Claire turned to me and said, "The line you read touched me."

"Really? I work in health care and it's important to stay focused on doing what is right for patients," I replied. The line seemed to be cerebral, not touching. I wondered why she had said that, but of course, I didn't ask her. The meaning of words is in the ear of the beholder as much as it is in the creator's mind.

We talked about my work in biotech and her work as a writer of historical fiction as we walked to the door.

Over the weeks, the class read poetry by Wordsworth, Hass, and Carson, and philosophy by Descartes, Plato, and Weil. As we debated, thought, mused, and wrote, Claire demonstrated an impressive breadth of knowledge and taught me so much.

One day, we decided to hang out outside of class. She suggested we go for a walk. "How about we meet at my house on Saturday morning?"

"Let me check with Elizabeth," I responded, having second thoughts on hanging out.

Was she suggesting friendship? A part of me hesitated. It took me a while before I warmed up to people. Initially, I was more comfortable with distance, and I felt that going to her house was a bit more than I bargained for in our first social interaction.

But another part of me jumped at the invitation. She'd intrigued me from the start. I told myself that I was just drawn to her as one would admire a mentor. Ultimately, I agreed to meet up with her at her house. I convinced myself that her neighborhood was in an ideal location to walk near the water and admire the scenery.

When Saturday came, I spent more time than usual getting dressed. After much contemplation, I decided to take the conservative route, and I chose black yoga pants with a baggy blue long-sleeve shirt. This look made me feel more comfortable, and it worked fine for a walk. I ignored the voice in my head that asked me why I even cared what I was wearing.

As I was driving to her place, I wondered what I might find. Given her unique style, I expected an artsy house, but her abode was a friendly, traditional home with a wraparound porch, light wood furniture, and views of the water. There was a vegetable garden and flowers of every color surrounding the porch.

As I went to ring the doorbell on the carved wooden front door, I hesitated. *Do I look okay in yoga pants? What are we going to talk about?* I was as nervous as I would have been going on a first date. Where was this coming from? An image of Elizabeth popped into my mind, and my stomach twisted. I looked back at my car, grateful it was a fast car, and imagined myself hotfooting it home.

Claire answered the door wearing a hoodie from Brown University, where she went to graduate school and earned her PhD in English.

"Hi. Come in." She stepped aside as I walked in.

The inside of the house was as down to earth and pleasant as Claire. Rugs, plants, books, and a piano filled the space. Her kitchen, full of hanging pots and pans, was in my line of sight, and I suddenly envisioned us making dinner together, our arms around each other.

Freaking bizarre!

I was spooked, and my stomach churned.

"Let's walk toward the water," Claire said, a kind smile on her face.

I thought about making up an excuse and heading home. Instead, I quietly said, "Okay."

Claire set a brisk pace with her long legs as she expertly led us across a busy road. I scurried across, trying not to get run over and struggling to keep up with her.

She did most of the talking on the walk. She spoke about her career and how she had enjoyed graduate school. She told me about her ex, Arthur, a painter, and about how much she loved kids. I was quiet, trying to make sense of the crazy feelings I felt for this woman—a woman who was certainly straight. What was wrong with me?

"Do you and Elizabeth have kids?" she asked.

Well, funny you should ask because I'm imagining having kids with you right now, I thought to myself. Thankfully, she didn't have telepathy.

How should I respond? Having children was a bone of contention between Elizabeth and me. And I didn't want to open up about my relationship.

"No. Long story. We have a beagle, though." I told her all about my adorable dog who spent most of the day curled up like a croissant in his bed.

As we continued to talk, my head swarmed with craziness. What would it be like to raise a family with Claire, to take our flock of kids on after-dinner walks and other outdoor adventures? Was she feeling this distressing connection, too? *Stop thinking these ridiculous thoughts!* I said to myself. *I am married, and she is straight.* I couldn't wait for our walk to end.

When we got back to her house, Claire said she enjoyed our walk and suggested we do it again, oblivious to having just hung out with a weirdo.

I had an urge to hug her and tell her, "Of course. Let's do this again." But mostly, I wanted to hightail it out of there and get back to my wife.

How could I think, even for one moment, about hurting Elizabeth? True, we had grown apart, but we had always been faithful and committed to each other and weathering the course and spending our lives together. But here I was fantasizing about building a life with another woman.

It's not that I didn't enjoy marriage or commitment—in fact, I loved it. Wearing my gold band was the greatest honor and privilege of my life. And after working toward marriage equality as a member of the LGBTQ+ community for years, I knew the privilege of our marriage. *How could I fail at something that so many of us put our hearts and energy into changing?*

Before I met Elizabeth, I dreamed of the day that I would be married and be able to build a life with someone. To build a family. It's not like I had expected marriage to be all sunshine and roses; Elizabeth and I would enjoy the good times together, and we would manage through the lows. I didn't rush into marriage too young, either. I was thirty-six when I married Elizabeth.

As I drove home, I tried to make sense of my nutty feelings. Why had Elizabeth and I become so disconnected? Why had I envisioned a life with someone else? What was wrong with me? My emotions were scrambled.

Maybe there was a simpler explanation. Maybe my feelings for Claire weren't real, but the result of a midlife crisis. At forty, I still had not had a child, and yet I had always wanted children.

But then again, maybe my feelings for Claire were real. People fall out of love with one person and in love with another person all the time.

I needed to get a handle on whatever was percolating deep inside me.

I got home, took a deep breath, and went into the house. Elizabeth sat on the sofa and smiled at me. "How was your walk?"

"Weird." I gave her a half smile back and avoided her gaze, retreating to the bedroom. There, I collected myself, while trying to push away the intruding thoughts about Claire.

Elizabeth was never the jealous type, which made it easier to tell her the truth—that I was attracted to Claire, but that I didn't want to hang out with her again. Elizabeth shrugged off my revelation, but I was shaken at my core.

I decided that my next order of business was to look for a marriage and family therapist. I found one who had availability to see me a few days later.

3

I arrived for my first counseling session with Dr. Hughes tired, with red eyes, my face downcast, and my mind foggy. I felt hopeful that I would be able to pull myself together and everything would go back to normal. But I also had a sense that my life was going to implode.

The office was warm and professional: a Persian rug, a painting of a relaxing ocean scene, and a light-pink leather chair that sat across from a honey-colored couch. Dr. Hughes wore a tailored navy suit and white linen blouse. She was a pleasant-looking woman with unadorned medium-length blond hair and brown eyes that looked sincere. On her finger was a simple gold wedding band that looked similar to my own. The walls held diplomas and photos of her husband and three children: two teenage boys and a girl who looked to be around ten years old.

After greeting me kindly, she pointed toward the couch, inviting me to sit down as she slid onto the light-pink chair. She informed me that everything we would discuss would be kept confidential unless there was a concern that I would be a harm to myself or others. Then she got down to business.

"What brings you in for counseling?"

The knot in my throat swelled to a lump. I looked around the room for Kleenex, not knowing how to explain the storm that was inside of me. I inhaled and took a deep breath before blurting, "My marriage is falling apart."

Dr. Hughes looked at me with interested eyes, waiting for me to continue. But I wasn't sure I wanted to.

"I am totally disconnected from my wife, and I have romantic feelings for a woman in my writing class. I think. I don't know." I gave her an overview of the walk I went on with Claire.

I glanced down at my hands, took another deep breath, and then peered up at Dr. Hughes, waiting for her to tell me how to put this genie back in the bottle and reconnect with Elizabeth. Instead, she peppered me with personal questions.

"Tell me about your marriage."

I gave her a brief chronological history.

"Tell me about your work."

I rattled off the major bullets from my résumé.

"Tell me about your family background."

"Uh. I was brought up by my mother, and I have an older brother. He lives in San Diego with his wife."

She said nothing, waiting for me to say more. But I didn't.

After a moment, she said, "Tell me about what is going on with the woman from your writing class."

"Nothing," I replied defensively. "I let my wife know I felt this attraction, and I haven't talked to Claire since the day we went on a walk. In fact, I skipped this week's class."

"Why, then, are you in such a distraught state? You haven't cheated on your wife," she said with a frown.

"But I have been thinking about Claire so much." *My heart is cheating.* I would have preferred for Elizabeth to have a one-night stand rather than to feel an emotional connection to someone else like the one I was feeling toward Claire.

Dr. Hughes squinted at me. "People who are in loving relationships have unexpected feelings for others all the time. Surely, you know this."

I felt like an idiot. I did not know this. It's not like I had been married before, nor did I blabber about my marriage to others or compare notes on what feelings are normal to feel. And fantasizing about a relationship with another woman felt wrong, scary, and out of control.

"Why do you worry that this sudden crush will make your marriage fall apart?"

Crush? I wanted to snap at her. Crushes are what I had in high school. With Claire, I had envisioned us cooking dinner, lady. This was unsettling, and I was freaked out.

I looked up at the ceiling. How do I explain? I couldn't make sense of the intensity of my feelings for Claire after one stupid walk. It seemed totally wacko to me, too. My gut was screaming red alert.

Finally, I responded, "Well, yeah there is more. I just turned forty, and I'm upset we don't have children. I've always wanted kids. Before we got married, Elizabeth and I had discussed having kids, along with other important topics. And according to our prenuptial plans, we should have had one by now."

At this point, I assumed that Elizabeth lacked my desire to be a parent. My desire to have a child was so strong that I had been saving fifty dollars a month in a college savings plan since I was twenty-two years old. Not having a child was a massive hole in my life.

"Why don't you have any children?"

That was my question, too. "I honestly don't know. We hardly even talk about it anymore. I bring it up every few months, and she doesn't seem to want to talk about it. So, then I drop it."

Suddenly, I felt the need to justify my relationship with Elizabeth to Dr. Hughes and added, "My marriage is good." At least I hoped it was. "She is a great partner, and we get along well."

I looked down. "I guess I don't know how to talk to Elizabeth. I'm a bad communicator. I've screwed up relationships all my life."

"How so?"

"Things fizzle out. The relationships last for a few years, and then I end them. I've done this in several long-term relationships."

"Where do you think this fear of intimacy comes from?" Dr. Hughes accused.

I froze. I never characterized it as a fear of intimacy. Instead, I made excuses as to why my relationships didn't work out. This appointment was becoming uncomfortable. It seemed easier to blame it on heredity. "Could be in my genes. My mom got pregnant with me with a married man. She never married my biological father, but she married four other men."

"Do you feel you're like your mother?"

"Not at all. I have lived my life very differently than she has." My mom is like a leaf in the wind; she follows her heart every time the wind blows a new direction, unlike me. I overanalyze everything.

That was all I was willing to share. I wasn't ready to discuss my roots. Doesn't everyone have a troubled childhood? Adversity is a universal human experience. The hard times made me better, anyway.

Nor did I want Dr. Hughes to see my mother as a bad person. She's not. Quite the opposite, actually. My mom's a bighearted hippie who loves life. A free spirit who wears tie-dye shirts and sandals as if every day were a 1960s music festival. When one of my friends complimented her necklace, she walked over to her, took it off her neck, and gave it to her.

The safest thing was to put a wall up so Dr. Hughes wouldn't pry further. "My marriage problems are not because of anything my parents did to me. It's on me."

Dr. Hughes asked, "When did you and your wife start to grow apart?"

Man, she was grilling me about the past and not giving me any answers. I sighed.

"Things started to go off track when we moved to Seattle. We seemed to blame it on the constant rainy weather." The lyrics of a Nirvana song played in my mind.

Focus, Sara, I snapped at myself.

"We've lived in our house for several months now, and we haven't hung any pictures and we can't even decide on a couch. We do our own thing. We don't even talk about important things like having kids."

"Do you get at each other?"

"No. We don't fight." And we didn't. Sure, we had little squabbles that created normal marriage tension, like having to negotiate who would have to fold the laundry because we both hated doing it. Or Elizabeth wanting a shoes-off house, but I wanted to wear my shoes in the house. We would compromise though, and in the latter case, she bought us both house slippers. Mine were loafers and hers were leopard print. Had I missed the signs that something was off because we didn't argue?

"Basically, we have a happy life. Only a month ago, for Christmas, we went to Costa Rica to visit her parents. Elizabeth was born there, and her entire family was there for the holiday. It was a good time."

I was either holding back or I was lying to myself. Something had been nagging at me about our relationship for a while. Our relationship started changing even before we moved to Seattle. When I asked Elizabeth if I could take the job, a voice inside of me whispered that if I did, we would end up getting divorced, but I had ignored it.

The threat of divorce must have been so real to the both of us that before we bought our current house, we decided not to put an offer on another house we liked because we heard the couple who owned it were selling it because they had gotten a divorce. The thought that this could foretell our own divorce scared us off. We didn't talk about this fear, and instead, decided to buy a brand-new house.

Why couldn't I open up to this therapist? How could she help me if I couldn't be open with her?

Dr. Hughes looked at me and said, "Have you thought about talking to your wife about having an open relationship? Some couples decide to open up their relationship when they feel attracted to others."

My chin nearly dropped to the floor.

"No. I haven't thought about having an open relationship."

Getting married, being monogamous for life, and building memories with my spouse is what I had envisioned, which was one reason that feeling so connected to someone else disrupted me. My disappointment revolved around us not having a child, and my stress was about losing my connection to Elizabeth. My head was spinning with this question. It had felt more like a suggestion.

Then, the fifty-minute session was over. Finally, I could leave.

I never did get to the underlying reason I came to see her—my worry was that there was something seriously wrong with me.

But what was wrong with me? Wasn't I supposed to open up in therapy, and to learn how to communicate my feelings? Why did this seem so impossibly hard to do? Dr. Hughes's questions felt like sandpaper rubbing on my skin. But I was still hopeful that Dr. Hughes could help me get to the bottom of it all. So I booked another appointment for the following week.

When I arrived at home, Elizabeth asked how my therapy session went. I conveyed to her what Dr. Hughes had said, and then I looked her in the eye and stupidly said, "She seemed to hint at an open relationship."

Elizabeth stayed poised, but her eyes revealed something else—hurt. We were both committed to fidelity and by sharing this statement, I had only created fear in her. I left the session more bonkers and unsettled than before. I was totally out of touch with myself. To try and make things better, I decided to take a stab at discussing the problems in our relationship with her. I remembered a conversation I had in Costa Rica at a New Year's Eve party. I was talking to one of her parents' friends when the lady mentioned how she and her husband spent a day every New Year discussing the health of their relationship and what changes they should make for the year ahead.

At the time, that nagged at me. I couldn't picture us doing that, and we didn't have shared goals. But now it seemed like the ideal thing to do.

"Let's talk."

"Okay," she said.

I sat down on the living room chair, and Elizabeth sat across from me. "I want this year to be different for our relationship. I'm worried that we're growing apart."

"I agree." Neither of us elaborated, but we happened to have a ski trip planned together for the following week, and I figured that we could pick up the conversation then.

I got up and hugged her. She hugged me back, which gave me momentary relief.

But when we got into bed later that night, our backs were turned away from each other. There was no communication about what was wrong or how we could fix it. I suppose we both assumed it would work itself out. On my end, I figured I just needed to banish my disruptive feelings for Claire.

4

A couple weeks later, I was back in class and willed myself to eject Claire from my mind.

The day before class, she'd texted, "How about another walk?" I ignored it. There was no way I was going on another walk with her after the first one sent me into a tailspin and to Dr. Hughes's office. When I walked into class, she smiled and said hello. I greeted her back, but I looked away, like she was a stranger, which left her with a bewildered look on her face. I then sat on the opposite side of the room to steer clear of her. Guilt welled up inside of me. *If I just avoid her, everything will go back to normal*, I thought, attempting to convince myself.

But of course, pushing down these emotions didn't work. They hadn't shrunk an inch. Pretending like she was a stranger was rude and weird. I chastised myself for being such a nincompoop. The mature thing to do was to be honest with her, after all, we were in the same writing community, for crying out loud. We could just go back to our collegial relationship, but life moves forward not backward.

I tried to gather my courage to face her after class, but it faded. I decided to text her instead. I wrote a few sentences, but I didn't send them. I rewrote the sentences a few more times, each revision becoming further evidence of my lunacy. In all fairness, Claire was a skilled writer, so proofreading was a good idea.

"It's best if we limit our interactions to class, nothing social. I felt an emotional connection to you during our walk, and I don't want to risk my connection growing," I wrote, and finally hit the send button.

Okay, no big deal, I said to myself, *hopefully, she will understand and maybe she'll even appreciate my over-the-top transparency.* She's straight, and I'm married. Mission accomplished. Back to normal life.

A couple of hours later, she still hadn't responded. I felt my stomach drop. I was embarrassed about my admission, but I also felt relief that I'd handled this head on.

Just be cool, I reassured myself, *act like this crush never happened.*

A few days later, she still hadn't acknowledged my text, which I considered a problem solved.

The next week, I saw her in class. I nodded courteously. She did the same. *Good*, I encouraged myself, *things will be back to normal soon enough.*

But I felt, or maybe imagined, subtle signals from her that gave the slightest hint at flirtation. Were her light eyes staring into my dark eyes as I read an excerpt out of a poem?

And so, when Claire wrote to me a couple of weeks later saying, "I felt a connection, too, and I've been thinking about you." I was shocked—as well as relieved that I wasn't delusional about that walk. I reasoned that she must have been touched by how I delivered my poems. That class, I was called on to read from William Wordsworth:

> *I listened, motionless and still;*
> *And, as I mounted up the hill,*
> *The music in my heart I bore,*
> *Long after it was heard no more.*

Maybe she found it endearing how I mumbled as I read the excerpts, my cheeks red in contrast to the dark business casual attire I wore.

Was I flattered and intrigued by her confession? No. I was downright scared and distressed—everything I had carefully built in my life, brick by brick, could come crashing down at any moment. Dread ran through my veins. *This is bad*, my brain yelled, *better keep a safe distance.*

I let Claire know that I wanted to protect my relationship with Elizabeth. She was on the same page. We agreed not to spend time together again socially. The seed of Claire was now firmly planted in my soul, but with self-discipline, I wouldn't water it.

When I got home, I told Elizabeth about the communication that had transpired between Claire and me, and that we had decided to keep a distance. And this time, I was direct with her, and told her that I was concerned about our marriage.

"We need to talk, Elizabeth. Our marriage is in trouble," I said, as I sat across from her at our dining room table. "I'm seriously worried. Having feelings for someone else seems like a huge red flag, and we need to do something about it."

Elizabeth looked at me directly, and then, after a long pause, she finally said, "I don't know what to say. But I wish you hadn't said anything to Claire." Yeah, I, too, regretted being honest with Claire. That was stupid. But at this point, I couldn't take it back. My concern was my relationship with Elizabeth, and my gut said that it was in jeopardy.

I responded defensively. "I was trying to do the right thing. I'm doing my best here."

"People don't need to tell their partners everything either," she responded. Her shoulders slumped.

My heart dropped. "I'm really sorry." There was no doubt in my mind that I had put a huge burden on Elizabeth with this information, leaving her to make sense of what was going on with me and us. We sat in silence as I searched for words that were not there.

The conversation hit a wall, so we discontinued it. Perhaps she was confident that we would be able to work through this bump in the road.

As the days went by, we didn't revisit the conversation, and our relationship became more disconnected and strained. And so, when she had to leave town a couple weeks later, I felt relieved. The break would provide me with space to clear my head and contemplate the things that were wrong with our relationship and my life.

My mind churned. The only thing that was clear was that although we talked about having kids before we got married, nothing had been decided during our four years together. I desperately wanted a child, and I dreamed of being a mother for as far back as I could remember. To me, it felt like being a parent would be the most important purpose of my life.

Whatever the reasons were in my head, it was the desire deep in my soul that propelled me forward.

The first few years of our marriage, I brought up having a child often. But Elizabeth, who was likely stressed at the mention of children and the pressure I put on her about it, would change the subject. When I get my mind set on something, I'm like a dog with a bone. Asking questions, listening, and understanding my partner's needs wasn't something I had figured out yet.

At first, I assumed she didn't want kids because she was focused on her career. She was five years younger than me and only a few years out of graduate school, so she didn't feel the same urgency that I felt at forty.

As time passed, I assumed it was because she didn't think I would be a good parent. I can be aloof, often with my head in the clouds. Once she said, "If we ever have kids, I am concerned that you would forget to pack the diaper bag with diapers." This was a fair point, but it stung.

Elizabeth was the organized, detailed one. When we went on vacation, she made a list of things that we needed to pack, while I quickly threw my items into the suitcase. "Do you have deodorant?" I asked on one trip. On another, I announced, "I forgot my socks. We need to find a store and buy some." I overlooked some of the most basic items, and I regularly needed to get toothbrushes from the front desk of whichever hotel I was staying at, having left mine at home. I even forgot my contacts when we went to Maui, and I had to get an eye exam at a LensCrafters on the island to get contact lens samples so we could go on a scuba diving excursion Elizabeth had scheduled a month before our trip.

But even worse was the fact that I worried she wasn't sure if she wanted to be married to me. What if she feared that a child would glue us together and it would be harder for her to leave me? Without that tie, she could take off more easily. This worry never left me. And if she left, I would be dried up and too old to have a child.

So, true to form, rather than asking her questions to try and resolve our dilemma, as intimately connected couples do, I quit talking to her about having kids. Although, I had recently started to look into fertility doctors and adoption online. Avoidance was easier—until it wasn't. And anyway, how could we decide on something as monumental as having and raising kids when we couldn't even decide how to furnish our new house?

My biological clock was ticking, and I was coming to a crossroads.

At the same time, I was still trying to kick out the vision of Claire and me hugging and cooking dinner together—our kids laughing and playing in the backyard while we worked as a team in the kitchen. Claire loved kids. My mind had added the kids in the backyard to the original vision.

I shook my head. What was I doing? These thoughts were crazy. I had to figure out how to get rid of these images. But the harder I tried to push these thoughts out, the more they irritatingly trespassed into my mind.

The solid, stable life I had built through the years of deliberate choices was going off the rails. Would things ever be the same?

Maybe I should move to another city and escape it all. Ah, the idea of running away brought me a huge sense of relief, like that of a glass of red wine at an unfamiliar social event.

5

"Maybe Elizabeth thinks of me as a ball and chain. Or maybe we aren't really compatible," I told Dr. Hughes during our next session. "We're from very different family backgrounds. She has lived in several countries and her family is sophisticated and highly educated. Lunch at her parents' house involves three courses and cloth napkins. My mother raised me and my brother while waiting tables." Dr. Hughes looked unimpressed at my admission.

"We don't even laugh at the same jokes anymore. In fact, Elizabeth only laughs when I'm not trying to be humorous, and she doesn't laugh when I am joking."

I was giving Dr. Hughes excuses and skirting around the real issue. "The worst thing is that she doesn't seem to share my strong desire to have kids. Or maybe she wants kids, but not with me."

"Have you thought about leaving her?" Dr. Hughes cut to the chase. "There are some issues in relationships, like having kids, that are often unresolvable."

Deep down, I was looking for permission from her to flee, but I did not like hearing this question. My chest was heavy. Was she saying that my marriage was ruined?

"I love Elizabeth," I responded, dizzy. If I couldn't make it work with a great person like Elizabeth, I couldn't last in a relationship with anyone.

Soon, she would be coming home from her trip to Costa Rica. I was too disoriented and stressed to stay in our house, so I decided to rent an Airbnb, where I could lament about getting old and how the New Year got off to a terrible start.

The decor was a far cry from our impeccably clean and spacious home—there was a kitchenette, a small bedroom, and a tiny bathroom with towels that had a slight detergent odor that made me worry that they hadn't been washed properly. The view was that of a parking area with broken glass bottles and a coffee shop across the street. The carpet looked like that of a '90s hotel room, and there was a discolored blue couch with a dip in the center. Still, this small, foreign space became a refuge from the omnipresent tension clouding my house. Being on my own soothed my insides.

I missed Elizabeth, but the urge to run away to my own space was overpowering. Being a coward, I emailed her while she was still out of town rather than have a heart-to-heart with her in person. I rationalized that writing my feelings down was a smarter way to express myself, instead of taking the risk of babbling words haphazardly, and that it would lead to better communication between us. My words come out on paper when I can't get them out of my mouth. At the very least, I was being open, which was something I had struggled with for a long time.

I structured the message as if it were a business email: a greeting, telling her how amazing she is, a bulleted list of the things that were wrong in our marriage, and next steps. The crux of it being that I needed a separation to figure things out. And that I would like to proceed with having a child, although I knew how unsure she felt about this. With hot tears running down my cheeks, I continued, "You would be better off without me anyway." I was doing her a favor, wasn't I?

My finger hovered over the send button. I stopped. There must be some way to save this.

I added, "I am open to counseling."

Finally, I closed my eyes and clicked send.

I wanted to crawl under a rock. But instead, I decided to call my mom, hoping that she would cheer me up.

She told me that it was a beautiful day in the Ozarks, where she lived.

I looked out the window and watched the pouring rain. The sky was gray, and the trees were barren. The world looked lifeless and spring seemed eons away. And while life also has seasons, I felt like I was going to be living in winter for a long time. Some people can experience the glory of winter, but I could not.

6

I decided to stop seeing Dr. Hughes. It was easier to blame her for not guiding me down a path that would instantly solve my problems than it was to take responsibility for my wrecking ball of behaviors. Elizabeth and I gave couples counseling a shot. She had been spinning, trying to make sense of my abrupt departure from our marriage, but she wanted to work on our problems. I, too, was wandering around in a maze that seemed like it had no exit.

Our therapist, who had teased blond hair and wore blouses that exposed her décolletage, looked like a soap opera star. She acted as if she was onstage when she counseled us. *Is she for real? Am I dreaming?* I looked over at Elizabeth to see if she had noticed, but she was taking notes as the therapist was talking.

The therapist's theatric demeanor continued to distract me. It was as if she was playing the part of a couples therapist, and we were in her play. It wasn't until later that I realized why the situation had seemed unreal. I was *derealizing*, a form of dissociation where things seem unreal. From time to time, all people zone out or shut down, which is disassociation, and I was disassociating by detaching from my emotions and my collapsing marriage.

Our therapist leaned forward and pointed to a diagram of a house. "Dr. Gottman, who is a renowned marriage researcher from the University of Washington, has spent decades researching what makes a marriage successful. He can even predict if a couple is going to get divorced within minutes just by observing them." She paused for what seemed like dramatic effect. "The Sound Relationship House is a framework to help improve your relationship. Just follow the principles that are connected to each level or floor of the house. Build Love Maps is the foundation. And that will be our first exercise—practice building love maps to better connect to each other. The focus here is for you to increase your positive experiences together."

As Elizabeth and I walked out of our first session, I said, "Doesn't she look like she's on *Days of Our Lives*?"

Elizabeth ignored my comment and said, "What did you think about what we talked about in the session?"

I shifted awkwardly from one foot to the other, searching for the right answer. Apparently, Elizabeth didn't think that our therapist was performing. "It was good . . ." I searched for more words, but none came to me. Elizabeth gave me her look, and I realized I was making things worse. So much for building love maps. I was numb, and neither of us understood that this emptiness was a symptom of trauma that was breaking through my internal barriers. My coping skills were not intact enough to keep it at bay.

We got into our separate cars, and I drove to my Airbnb and Elizabeth drove to our house. Self-loathing and self-limiting beliefs grew with every mile I drove.

Like my parents, I am incapable of sustaining a commitment, I told myself. *I am selfish, and I cannot give enough to a partner*, I chastised myself. *I'm a real piece of work and belong on my own*, I convinced myself.

Despite the bad start, we continued to go to our therapy sessions. Elizabeth didn't want the marriage to end, and she was willing to try everything possible in order to save it. I was disoriented and ambivalent. She pressed me and said, "You have one foot in and one foot out."

"You're right." I owned up to it, although maybe I was being unconstructively candid. My emotions were all swirled up. I was having a hard time making heads or tails out of them. "But I do have one foot in, and I'm trying." I didn't want to give up, and so I committed to staying focused. During our next few sessions, I kept myself in check, especially when I felt like I was in an awful play.

The therapist directed us back to The Sound Relationship House, but we were more consumed with discussing our problems. Claire continued to run laps in my head, and I was still more connected to work than home.

I blocked out our therapist and looked at Elizabeth. "I don't get it. I go to work and I come home every day around five thirty. I pretty much do whatever you want to do. I arrange nights out, and I go wherever you want to go on vacation."

"You are there but you aren't really there. Your head is in work or off to some other place," she replied.

"You are the most important person in my life. My inner world and work are important, too, and I need to spend time in those places."

At least we were being open, but we were more or less going in circles. In between sessions, I reflected on what Elizabeth had said, and I took some things to heart. I decided to make some changes, like keeping my phone away during our meals moving forward. I permanently adopted this behavior. But I also contemplated what I should do about having kids, and so, I went ahead and made an appointment at a fertility clinic without discussing it with Elizabeth.

I believed that most of our problems were solvable, but I couldn't see a way for us to fix things unless she agreed to have children. Any route of having a baby was fine with me. She could have one, I could have one, or we could adopt.

During our last session, the therapist gave up The Sound Relationship House and simply asked us what we wanted to talk about. She had stopped performing.

I looked at Elizabeth, and I told her that I had made a fertility appointment. "I must take steps toward having a child."

"I'm open to a family after we repair our marriage," she declared. This was the hill we were going to die on.

I was skeptical, but she had been putting a serious effort into therapy, and she was committed to getting through our rough patch. Her notebook was filled with notes.

Still, this seemed chicken and egg. Wasn't having kids the route to fixing our marriage? How long would it take for us to get on track? What if we continued down this path for another year or two, and we couldn't work things out? It could be too late. I wanted to have kids immediately.

At the same time, I knew that Elizabeth was right. It didn't make any sense for us to bring a baby into an unstable marriage.

I announced, "I'm forty years old. I can't wait until after our marriage is fixed. I don't know how long that will take or if we will be able to fix it."

She nodded. Her face drooped with sadness. It was a no-win situation for her. "Let's file for divorce." She kept her composure. The therapist didn't say a word as Elizabeth and I left her office.

My insides were a tornado.

I wanted to puke. My stomach burned and my brain was on fire. The future looked bleak.

7

I waited for the relief to come, but it didn't. I had failed Elizabeth and our marriage. Swallowing my tears, I called my mother.

My mother is the type of person who takes time to admire flowers. She listens to the birds and touches the trunks of trees. She keeps dark chocolate Hershey kisses in her purse. She has never judged me, and despite my being resentful of how she raised me, we've remained close. I can talk to her about anything. She seems to understand things about being human that I don't: the human experience is complex and nuanced. Black and white, good or bad, right or wrong are often too simplistic. Humans make mistakes, sometimes repeatedly, until we figure out our way out of the maze. But we also have an important choice to make—we either learn and grow from our mistakes or we don't.

I didn't possess this wisdom; I was either *good* or *bad*. And after my marriage failed, I deemed myself bad. And when you add that I wanted to be with another woman, I became a shameful monster.

"What are you up to, Mom?"

"Not much," she chirped. "I'm watching the birds." I could hear Bob Dylan playing in the background, and I wondered if she was stoned, which would have been typical.

"How are you?" she asked.

"Not good. Elizabeth and I split up," I murmured, choking up. "Can you come visit me?"

"Yes," she said immediately. She was usually playful, but she said this in an uncharacteristically serious tone.

She was on the next flight to Seattle.

My mom arrived wearing rainbow tie-dye leggings and carrying a bright-purple suitcase that smelled like cigarette smoke. She bounced up to my car, which was parked outside of the airport. My mother was only five foot tall and weighed ninety-seven pounds, but she captured attention.

"Hi!" she yelled joyfully, as if the world was a perfect place.

As I watched her bob over to my car, I wondered how she could be so cheerful when life sucked so much.

"Thanks for coming," I said, as I walked over to her and gave her an obligatory quick hug. She squeezed me tightly. Hugging her had always felt awkward, but I usually got away with giving her a one-armed hug. She was like an excited puppy: she was too expressive, too emotional, and too affectionate for my comfort.

I took her suitcase and put it in the trunk.

On the car ride home, my mind was elsewhere. I nodded my head patiently as she rattled on about how great her flight was, how nice it was to look out the window, and how the lady next to her was also coming to Seattle to visit her daughter.

When we arrived at the Airbnb, I wondered if she would notice the stains on the couch. I had failed to scrub them out when I first moved in, and keeping my house, my office, and my car excessively clean was important to me. But as she glanced around the Airbnb, she smiled at me and said contentedly, "This is a nice place." I knew my mom meant it. She was an eternal optimist who saw the silver lining in everything, despite her difficult life.

When I applied for financial aid for college as a teenager, I sifted through my mom's tax records, and I discovered that her highest earning year was just under thirteen thousand dollars, which was under the federal poverty level.

And yet, she did not see herself as *poor*; she was grateful for what we did have. My mother never took advantage of the free lunch program at my school. And when she got an extra twenty-dollar bill at the grocery store once, she handed it back to the cashier, letting her know that she had given her too much change. When my school held donation drives, she would send me in with canned goods and holiday gifts. She was generous to a fault.

She never pursued child support from my father—a wealthy entrepreneur who made millions as a real estate developer and business owner—although he could have easily afforded it. My father was basically a sperm donor who I had only met a few times. The last time I saw him was when I was twenty-one. He died a few months before I walked out of my marriage.

I was bitter with my mom about the bad choices she continued to make in her life. I was always nagging her to quit smoking. I told her not to loan the neighbor any money because she would never see it again. I reminded her not to forget to pay the utility bill. And although it had been hard for my mom to eke out a living, she regularly told me how proud she was of my professional success.

It's not that she was incapable. She was quite savvy. She had learned how to navigate the world of poverty creatively, solving problems with something as simple as duct tape. When I was eleven, we spent a summer living in a tent, and my mom used duct tape to cure a hole that had formed. And she turned strips from that the same roll of tape into a fly trap in our tent. These were our homeless months, but they were also some of the best times we spent together. I played outside every day in the creek with the other kids at the campground, and we cooked our meals over an open fire with music filling the night air. We would remove debris from our clothes with duct tape as we left the campground to go watch a play in the park. All I could see at the time was poverty, not all the riches.

It hadn't occurred to me that my mom's life may be richer than mine. There was too much dormant anger about to break through the surface.

When she unzipped her suitcase, she pulled out environmentally hazardous plastic grocery bags and handed them to me. Her eyes lit up like rainbow lights on a Christmas tree. "All of the answers are in here," she said as she looked at me.

My eyebrows furrowed in confusion. "Answers to what?"

"Your life." Her eyes sparkled as if she knew all the secrets of the universe.

What is she talking about? I humored her by pulling out the contents of the bag, spreading them on the little round dining table. There were notes, greeting cards, and poems I had saved since childhood. In her efforts to help me, she had gathered these letters and relics, which had been aging in a box in the garage, and brought them to me.

Why had she brought these? How could this help? I played along and continued to sift through them. I smiled when I saw a drawing of a rose that an old boyfriend had drawn for me.

And then, shock. I stiffened. My eyes focused on a cutout from a newspaper article from 1990 with the headline "Suspect Surrenders in Fatal Shooting of Oceanside Girl." How horrific and how heartbreaking for her family. I shut my eyes.

The article went on to report the drive-by shooting of Gloria Torres, a fourteen-year-old, at Alberto's Mexican Food on Redondo Drive and North River Road in Oceanside, California. Gloria was there with three friends when the shooting took place, according to the article.

My body pulsed and throbbed as I read the story. I lived in the same neighborhood where the shooting happened, and I was only a few months younger than Gloria. Dizzy and shaky, I felt pain well up in my chest, and a burning blazed across my torso with intensity.

Then, as quick as if I had shut off a light switch, my entire body stilled. I was as calm as morning lake water. Too calm. I felt nothing. If someone had walked by and punched me in the gut, I wouldn't have felt a thing. My head reeled, and I felt bewildered. Why had everything in my body shut down?

I rummaged through the rest of the bag frantically. There were more notes from friends, another greeting card with a cute kitten on the cover, but nothing explained the significance of the article.

I unfolded another letter. This one was from Fran, an old classmate, and it had a date written on it. It was from the week after Gloria had died. "Hey, girl. I hope you are okay after everything. I am so sorry about Gloria. I'm here for you." She had underlined *so sorry* and signed her name with hearts.

Friend? Gloria Torres? Maybe I could locate Fran and ask her what she remembered. It was so long ago, though, how would I find her? Somebody had to give me answers.

I felt as if I was in the twilight zone. I quickly squirreled through the rest of the pile of letters, looking for anything else that might help explain this mystery. Finally, near the bottom of the pile, I found two letters in my handwriting. I had written these to Gloria after she died. The first letter said, "Dear Gloria, I miss you so much. I am sorry I ran and left you on the ground. It should have been me that was shot. I will miss you forever." The second letter was me reiterating that I missed her. Next, I read a poem I wrote titled "Death" dated November 25, which is my birthday, from the same year that Gloria died:

> Death will be at the strangest times.
> Life will breathe its last breath.
> Death will be dark and dull.
> It will be as fast as a ray of light.
> There you will lay asleep.
> Not knowing what happened.
> That is death in the worst way.

Man, I was in a dark place as a teenager. What the hell! I couldn't remember a thing about her or her death. Was I such a screwed-up kid that I imagined I was there? Or had I forgotten?

My mother must know.

I looked at her. She was nibbling on a peanut butter cookie she had grabbed from her purse, oblivious to what I was reading.

"Mom," I squeaked. "Did you read this stuff?"

"No, I just grabbed them before I came. Figured you must have saved these things for a reason." I thrust the article and the letters toward her for her to read.

"Did you know about this?"

She nodded as she read. "This shooting is why we moved."

"What! Did I know her? I can't even picture her! Do you remember her?" None of this was making sense.

"It's so hard to remember. I was working a lot." The truth was that she didn't know much about what went on in my life during this time. She was rarely home. She spent most nights waiting tables at the Pizza Hut, and on many of her days off, she'd be out of town visiting my stepfather, Earl. She and Earl were separated at the time. I thought we had moved because they got back together—not because of a shooting.

Still, she had to remember something. Was she so oblivious about my life that she didn't even know who my friends were? There was no way that she was going to help me get to the bottom of this.

I had absolutely no memory of the incident. I searched every corner of my brain, but nothing came up. The only facts I had were that the girl and I lived in the same neighborhood, and we were a few months apart in age.

Acid churned in my stomach. A neighborhood girl had been shot at the Mexican restaurant down our street. Had I witnessed the death of a friend? I had no clue. But this girl's murder shocked me. Even if I wasn't there, a neighbor being shot down the street could have impacted me. My body was still numb as my mind swam.

Maybe my brother remembered something. My mom looked over my shoulder as I texted him, "Do you remember a shooting at Roberto's in 1990?"

He responded that he did remember, but he didn't know if I had been there when it happened. He's almost five years older than me, so we didn't know much about what was happening in each other's lives back then.

One thing was clear—I needed to see another therapist. One that specialized in trauma because for all I knew, this event could have left a huge imprint on my life, and it might account for some of the distance I kept in my relationships. I was hopeful that a trauma specialist might help me unearth this memory and help bring me a sense of peace.

I shared this with my mom.

"Why would you want to go back into the past?" she asked me. "I leave the past in the past."

Was she right? This was the conventional wisdom. I debated whether I should keep the past in the past or face my demons.

A quote by Dag Hammarskjöld from a bracelet I wore when I was younger popped into my mind: "The longest journey is the journey inward." Did I want to go on a long journey inward? Did I want to dig into the depths of myself and deal with my issues from the root cause? Perhaps it was best to just scratch the surface and find a quick fix to Band-Aid the turmoil.

Ultimately, I decided to face my demons and lecture my mom a bit.

"First of all, leaving things in the past doesn't work. It will continue to seep out in different ways, like substance abuse." This was a passive-aggressive bullet fired directly at her. When I was in elementary school, during her lowest point, my mother had been a crystal meth addict.

My addiction was my career. I got hooked on receiving external validation of my worth, so I threw myself into my work. I was too busy to have to get real with myself.

"Second, shutting out the bad feelings keeps the good feelings out as well." I remembered this insight from a Brené Brown clip, although I hadn't grasped the concept yet.

My mom looked at me blankly as I continued wagging my finger at her.

"Third, I will pass trauma on to others if I don't work out my stuff." Nobody needed to tell me that trauma is intergenerational and spreads like the plague. I wanted kids and would walk through fire to keep them mentally, emotionally, and physically safe.

"Last, I have to change to make a relationship work. I keep screwing up. And I don't even understand why or what it is I am doing wrong."

My mom considered all of this for a minute. "You could just take a pill."

If I were a dog, I would have growled at her, but I bit my tongue and stewed over all the substances she had abused as quick fixes: cigarettes, alcohol, drugs . . .

Silence hung in the air. Finally, my mom said, "Let's go do something fun."

Relieved by the idea of a distraction, we hopped in my car and headed to the Chihuly Museum, where we were transported into an enchanting world of whimsical glass sculptures and gardens. It was amazing how only an hour earlier the world had felt dark, and now it was filled with beauty and wonder. While we were out, I grumbled, "How are you so happy all the time?"

She said, "I take the good with the bad and the ups with the downs."

8

Things formed a new kind of normal in my Airbnb. I woke up for work around six every day and made my bed. After I got ready, even though I had lost my appetite for food, I would sit down to choke down breakfast, oatmeal and fruit or Greek yogurt, while I penciled my daily to-do list.

I strolled across the parking lot to the little coffee shop and said hi to Niran, the friendly barista who greeted me by my name. I clutched my trusty coffee cup as I went into the office. I acted as if everything was great, and I buried myself in my work.

I made myself busy to keep from ruminating over my split from Elizabeth and to keep from daydreaming about Claire. I bombed. I was initially drawn to her mind, but now even her walk captivated me. It was graceful like a ballerina's, but it was also brisk because she had important places to go. Although I maintained distance from her in class, occasionally, our eyes would fuse together. I would look away as my chest simultaneously warmed and panicked.

I was in a full-blown existential crisis. Outside of work, I occupied myself by reading psychology books for clues about what was wrong with me, and I read philosophy trying to make sense of life. When I couldn't focus, I watched movies. If I sat still, I would bounce back and forth between shame and worry, waiting for numbness to anesthetize my turbulent emotions.

I felt grateful when my longtime friend Mirielle, who lived in New York, told me she was coming to visit. Mirielle was a classy lady from a prominent French family and had grown up in Paris. Her elegant French accent made me want to wrap a silk scarf around my neck when in her presence. The ways of the United States took some adjustment for her. "It was strange to drink out of a paper cup," she said once. "In Paris, we take our time to drink our coffee. Not walk with it in a paper cup."

Now I had to tell her she would be sleeping on my stained couch.

I called her a few days before her arrival and told her that she would be staying with me in an Airbnb. "Elizabeth and I have split up, and I'm no longer living at home. There isn't a guestroom, but there is a fold-out couch."

"Certainly," she said graciously. "I'm coming to see you and will support you in any way I can."

What a huge relief it was to have her visit for the weekend. We went to a professional soccer game, ate at restaurants, and walked around the city, chatting away. Her company allowed me to momentarily forget my sucky personal life.

Not wanting to burden her with my stuff, I tried to keep our conversations light. I told her that the company I worked for had just been bought by a large biotech company. She looked concerned, possibly worrying I would be laid off, but I reassured her that my finances were solid, so solid that I might be in financial shape to retire early should I wish to do so.

She broke out in a huge smile, but my expression remained glum. I felt lousy sharing this, as if my life had so little inherited worth, I had to bring up something of external value—money. Despite my financial situation, I felt worthless because I'd screwed up my marriage. This shame was swallowing me so wholly that when we went out, I asked her to dine with me at the bar rather than at a table where, sitting side-by-side, I could avoid eye contact.

After Mirielle left my lovely Airbnb, I could barely force myself to eat or get out of bed.

My pants were getting loose and starting to hang off me. An apocalyptic nightmare woke me up at three in the morning one night, and I had to change out of my pajamas because they were drenched in sweat. I was swamped with fear.

PART II

As long as you keep secrets and suppress information, you are fundamentally at war with yourself. The critical issue is allowing yourself to know what you know. That takes an enormous amount of courage.
—Dr. Bessel van der Kolk

9

A few months after I walked out of my marriage, I ambled into Janis's office. She is a therapist who specializes in trauma. As much as I was frustrated to find myself in therapy, I knew I was lucky to have access to mental health care through my insurance and resources. It's a privilege that so many people don't have.

With its pale-yellow walls, four mismatched chairs, a water dispenser with tea bags, handmade ceramic mugs, and some magazines, the waiting area of my new therapist's office was cozier than the one in Dr. Hughes's office. A young woman with black-dyed hair sat in one of the chairs looking at her hands. She never looked up.

After making a cup of ginger tea, I sat down and glanced around. Three abstract paintings hung on the walls, colorful but nondescript, almost like a Rorschach test, I thought.

The door to the therapist's office opened, and a fit, hipster-looking middle-aged woman with short red hair and olive eyes motioned me to come in. Her energy engulfed me like a warm hug.

"I'm Dr. Levin, but you can call me Janis," she smiled as she spoke, putting me at ease. "Please come in."

The room was simple and comfortable. No diplomas, even though she had a PhD degree in clinical psychology from a top university. On the other side of the desk was a lemon-colored comfy couch, a light wooden square table at its side, and two brown leather chairs that faced each other.

Janis motioned for me to take a seat in one of the chairs, and she sat across from me in the other. We were sitting closely enough for us to feel engaged, but far enough apart that I didn't feel threatened.

She began by telling me that everything that was said between us was confidential, except of course, if I was a harm to myself or to others.

"The saying in graduate school is that we got in this line of work to heal ourselves or someone we love." She informed me that she had experienced trauma herself, which created an immediate connection. I was in the right place.

"So, what brings you in?"

Now that I was feeling relaxed, I shared with her that my marriage had fallen apart, and that my mom had brought these childhood letters that suggested that I may have witnessed a shooting of a friend, but that I did not remember.

I glanced up, expecting to see a surprised look on her face as I told her about the girl who died and my lack of memories of the event. Instead, she looked at me calmly, like she had heard a story like this a thousand times.

"And what is your goal for therapy?"

I paused for a while, reflecting on the question. Should I tell her my goal was to figure out which end was up? This seemed glib. I confessed that what I truly wanted was to figure out how to make a relationship last, how to be a good partner and a good mother—if I would ever be lucky enough to have a child. "I've always wanted a family," I told her. "A happy family."

She nodded, indicating that this was attainable, then provided me with an overview on trauma.

"Exposure to trauma, especially during childhood, has an impact on the development of the brain and the nervous system," she explained. "Which can manifest as hypo-arousal or hyper-arousal. Symptoms of hypo-arousal are things like numbness, boredom, and emptiness, and hyper-arousal can include difficulty sleeping, angry outbursts, and anxiety."

She took her time to make sure I was tracking.

"Kids adapt to toxic stress in their environment by adopting defense mechanisms. Examples of this can be isolation, denial, or acting out. And they scan their environment for danger. Hypervigilant."

I nodded.

"Another way a child will self-protect is through repression, especially if an event was too terrifying for the child to cope with, or if a child doesn't receive adequate support when something horrific happens. In other words, forgetting is a normal response to trauma. The term for this is dissociative amnesia. It protects the child from the disruption and pain that the event caused, which is useful as it helps them go about their life."

She paused, and a long silence hung in the air until I spoke. "This makes sense so far."

Janis searched my eyes kindly before continuing . "But eventually, even decades later, things we repress can resurface and cause debilitating psychological and behavioral problems. The person's overly sensitive stress-response system may become overwhelmed, which causes the individual to get even more easily triggered into a flight, fight, or freeze response."

When I felt skittish in relationships, I often fled by clamming up and detaching. Had I been triggered?

Janis continued. "People can live a long time with previous traumatic events staying dormant before they break through. This often happens in one of three ways: when the person is ready to deal with things, something happens that cracks the person open, or the mind gets tired of suppressing the past."

"Okay. Can you tell me more about triggers?"

"A trigger," she explained, "is when something like a sight, a sound, an emotion, or a smell reminds someone of the past, and they overreact to that stimulus. The telltale sign is when an individual has a disproportionate reaction to something, like yelling in rage or shutting down. The rational cerebral cortex, the one with the executive functioning capabilities, goes offline, and the survival instinct of the old brain stem takes over."

It sounded like a person could get out of control in this situation.

After chewing on this concept for a few minutes, it made sense. "I think I get it. I think I got triggered when Elizabeth came home late. The stimulus was the clock ticking. My response was sheer terror that something bad had happened to her." As a kid, I worried about my mom dying, and I had those same fears with Elizabeth.

"Last year, when she got home almost an hour late from work, I had this graphic image that filled my head of her car turned upside down in a ditch." My heart began pounding in my throat as I recalled this. "I called her phone, but she didn't answer. The minutes moved slowly, and I dreaded that she was in the hospital or worse, dead. I tried to focus on making dinner, but, instead, I paced the living room like a lion in a cage. When she finally walked through the door, my blood pressure was through the roof, and I snapped at her." This was also a familiar childhood scenario: my mother chronically came home late.

"Exactly. You had a disproportionate bodily and emotional reaction," Janis confirmed.

"So how do I fix all of this?" I was ready to roll up my sleeves and solve this immediately. I wanted to rip out and eliminate all of these issues from the root, not just clip them.

She raised her eyebrows. "I believe you will be in a very different place in a few years. But you need to process any unresolved trauma first."

Years! She clearly didn't know me, or how intensely I worked toward my goals. Little did I know that this journey would bring me to my knees many times, and how I would be shattered into multiple messy pieces to be rebuilt.

I nodded, grateful. This woman struck a nerve. Something had been off inside of me for a long time, and I trusted that Janis would be able to guide me through it.

She leaned forward and locked eyes with me. "I need your informed consent." She described common approaches she uses and the risks involved. "Therapy often increases symptoms in the short term. Basically, things often get worse before they get better."

I consented and, arrogantly, believed that I would be able to work out my stuff in no time. I would kick my baggage in the ass.

She gave me an assignment to do. I had to create a timeline of my life with all the significant things I remembered, good or bad.

"Sure thing." I thanked her and left her office eager to get started.

Instead, I procrastinated on my timeline homework, and I started to psychoanalyze myself. I must have lived my life to avoid being outside of my *window of tolerance*, a concept I read about online: when a person is out of their comfort zone, they go from hyper-arousal to hypo-arousal. Work must have been a coping tool during these times, a distraction from the uncomfortable feelings, and it worked so well that even my colleagues joked that I never seemed stressed. Ha!

10

The night before I was to see Janis again, I stared at my blank legal pad. Finally, my hand started jotting down bullet points, while I sat in the dip on the blue couch.

I started with the earliest memories, and I worked my way to present day. Memories started to emerge from me like popcorn popping, but writing them down zapped my energy.

One of the early memories that popped into my mind was one when I was three years old.

I had lost my stuffed Smurf, my constant companion. It fell out of my hands when I was climbing onto the back bench seat of my mom's old car.

As she pulled out of the parking garage, I cried, "My Smurf!"

"We'll get you another one," she said, while singing along to Neil Diamond's "Forever in Blue Jeans." But a new Smurf never came.

Even though it had happened years ago, I still remembered that the car smelled like an ashtray, a smell that has always revolted me.

I wasn't sure why that memory had popped into my mind. It was just a ridiculous stuffed animal. Should I even bother to share it with Janis? I decided to include it, and I added a couple dozen more memories, bad and good.

Looking over the list, I was filled with regret over the incredible people I had lost touch with over the years. I blamed it on my career, which it had forced me to move from city to city, and I felt like the archetypal, albeit corporate, rolling stone that gathered no moss.

I remembered my sorority sisters, whom I had laughed and hung out with throughout college. People occasionally teased me about being in a sorority, but these amazing ladies were family. I thought of the professional friends I had made after college; they were all great people who I learned from in the office. We enjoyed Super Bowl parties and happy hours. I recalled the first group of leaders that mentored me and taught me about leadership, and how to better equip myself to enable and empower my own team members to achieve their goals.

I thought of the people I dated and cared about but had walked out on. The family members I had walled off, including my own brother. We spoke on the phone a couple times a year, and we saw each other only about once a year. When we did see each other, we got along well enough, and I enjoyed being around him and his wife. They had been married for a long time and her parents and siblings were fun to be around, especially for their festive Sunday-night family dinners. My brother and I kept things to the present and didn't talk about our past.

I thought of my precious dog, Parker, a chocolate lab mix that I left with my ex, Angela, after we broke up because I had to travel for work too often to take care of him. Parker was given to me when he was two weeks old by a pregnant woman who I randomly ran across in a grocery store parking lot. She waddled up to me as I was getting into my car and told me that his mother had a litter of puppies in her garage and had left him. His eyes weren't even opened yet, and he couldn't walk. Having a soft spot for abandoned beings, I cradled him in the palm of my hand and took him home and bottle fed him. The irony was not lost on me that I later left him.

Now what? Should I start reaching out to people? Reactivate my Facebook? My last photo and update were from almost ten years ago.

While the good memories created longing and regret, the bad memories seemed to affect me very little—that's how flat my emotions were—and I was able to jot them down quickly.

That is, except for the time my hand strangely stopped working. I found I couldn't write anything down from after I was seventeen on the same piece of paper as my childhood years. As I stared down at the ample empty space on the blue-lined legal pad, my brain could not make my hand continue. I shook it and scolded myself to keep writing, but my hand wouldn't listen.

I flipped to a new sheet of paper and titled it *adult*, and my hand easily started writing all the key memories from my adulthood. I was unsure what Janis was going to do with my timeline, but I forced myself to trust her enough to follow her lead. I hoped she could help me get to the bottom of my intimacy and commitment issues.

I later learned that when I went to college, I had severed and banished my childhood memories to the extent that I was unable to write them on the same piece of paper as adulthood. Janis explained that I had segregated my child self from my adult self, and that we would need to work on integrating them back together. She shared a quote from Carl Jung: "Wholeness is not achieved by cutting off a portion of one's being, but by integration of the contraries." I had no idea what that meant but admitted to her that I felt cut off from parts of myself.

11

In high school and in college, I had boyfriends who I enjoyed spending time with. These relationships were simple and fun. It didn't strike me as odd that my friends were more into their boyfriends, because I had a full life between school and work.

Eric and I were a couple for most of my time in college. We met on our first day, after we had both arrived on campus our freshman year. Bright-eyed and bushy-tailed, a group of girls and I walked to our first house party, the first of many, and we ran into a group of guys that were walking to the same party. Our groups merged, and Eric and I walked together. We talked about where we were from, and what we planned to study. He was from Wisconsin, and his pale-blue eyes had a striking contrast to his black hair.

We entered a two-story white house through the side door. After paying five dollars at the door to get in, we received a red Solo cup and headed down the rickety stairs to the basement, where Eric and I continued our conversation. There were kegs of beer and a forty-gallon trash can full of *wop*, a mixture of fruit juice and grain alcohol.

Eric was a polite, handsome guy who was on the football team, and at the end of the night, he asked me out on a date. The following Friday night, he cooked us dinner in his dorm room. He made an impressive, respectable dinner of pasta and vegetables using a microwave and a hot pad.

If we didn't see each other, we'd speak daily. We occasionally went to church together and spent several holidays with his family. After a few years together, we assumed we would get married and have kids, but one night, when I was twenty-one, at a toga party, it all changed.

Lauren, a girl from another sorority, walked up to me. She didn't say a word but took my hand and walked me outside. We were both tipsy from the plastic cups full of beer. As we wobbled over to a bench away from the rest of the crowd, she stared at me, and I smiled, awkwardly. She then leaned toward me and passionately kissed me. It was electrifying. It felt as if I was watching a black-and-white television in color for the first time. It knocked me off my feet.

This attraction didn't totally surprise me.

When I was in high school, living in rural Missouri, I got a job at the Lake of the Ozarks Marriott resort. When the summer season arrived, a mass of interns came from over a dozen schools around the world. I was assigned to show them around. After work, we would hang out at parties together or at Woody's, a local bar with a shuffle board and jukebox.

One intern, in particular, drew me into her orbit. Her name was Phoebe. Outgoing with a magnetic personality, she was from Minnesota and was the president of her sorority (which I would later join). I admired her fashion, her sense of humor, and even how she looked in the work uniform we all wore. She somehow made her army-green pants, bright-orange button-up shirt, and name tag look cool. She rolled up her shirt sleeves, unbuttoned two buttons below the collar, and accessorized.

She was on a six-month internship, longer than the summer rotation most of the other interns were on. Once summer ended and the rest of the interns returned to their universities, Phoebe and I began hanging out more. I followed her around like a puppy, so she must have assumed I looked up to her.

But on my seventeenth birthday, I let my inner party animal out. Phoebe and I drank boxed wine and chased it down with shots of tequila. I'd drank alcohol before, but nothing like this. I woke up dazed, a pounding headache settling in. I was in her apartment, in her bed, and she was next to me. We were both still wearing our clothes from the night before. She opened her eyes, and we looked at each other. My chest heated. I jumped out of bed, freaked out by my attraction to her.

It wasn't until the electric kiss with Lauren that I admitted to myself that I might be gay. It was confusing, though. Maybe it was a result of the alcohol, which was the common denominator both times. I thought that if I abstained from liquor, the feelings might go away. But that didn't ring true. I needed time and space to figure things out. I needed to talk to Eric.

"Lauren and I kissed last night. What if I'm gay? I need to be on my own to figure it out. I am so sorry," I told him the next day.

He looked like a deer in headlights. "Do you think this is a phase?" He said this as if I were a toddler who was being potty trained.

"I hope so." My chin quivered a bit. "I want to have a family in the future." This was the early '90s, and I had come of age in a small town. I didn't know any gay people, and I also didn't know it would be possible to have a family in a same-sex relationship.

I felt terrible, but I also felt impatient. I wanted to uncover my sexual orientation before I ended up getting married. Eric took our breakup like a champ, and six months later, we were giving each other relationship advice. He had started seeing one of Lauren's sorority sisters, while I was secretly dating Lauren.

Clank, click, clank. I'd hear pebbles hitting my bedroom window late at night. Cell phones didn't exist yet, so we couldn't text, and a call to our shared house phone would have woken everyone up. Through my window on the second floor of the sorority house, I could see Lauren standing below. She would come over late at night after everyone had gone to sleep. I would sneak her into my room until early the next morning before sneaking her back out before everyone woke up. We both would bring male dates to any event where a date was customary.

Part of me hoped I would get rid of this deplorable curse, but the other part of me felt pulled to explore the intoxicating feelings I felt with Lauren. *How could this be wrong if it felt so right?*

I needed to tell someone to lighten the weight of my secret. I called my mom.

"I have something important to tell you." I could hear music and her friends laughing in the background. *Seriously Mom, it is still morning on a Sunday.*

She waited but the words were clogged in my throat. "What is it?"

My sweaty hands wanted to hang up the phone. "Nothing."

"What is it?" she asked again.

"Guess." I slapped my hand on my forehead. *Guess!* Why did I say that?

"You're quitting school?" No. "You got a dog?" No. "You're quitting your sorority?" "No, and I would have to quit the sorority if I got a dog. We aren't allowed to have pets in the sorority house."

She gave up guessing. I took a deep breath. "I might be gay."

"That's a relief. I thought you were about to say that you're pregnant."

It was a relief that my mother had not freaked out on me. I didn't have the guts to tell anyone else in my extended family, so I asked my mom to inform them if she thought they needed to know.

My mother was the most liberal person in my Midwest Catholic family. My grandmother, my aunts, and my uncles were relatively conservative. To some of them, homosexuality was a sin—God's curse. I worried they might ostracize me, but they didn't. Still, the vibe at times was, as the saying goes, "love the sinner, hate the sin."

When Elizabeth and I got married, only a few people from my extended family came, while her whole family attended. A couple of my aunts did not even bother to decline my wedding invitation. They didn't simply check the "no" box on the RSVP card and stick it back in the mail in the enclosed stamped envelope. Instead, they ignored that I was getting married. This hurt. However, I was grateful to my mom, my brother, my sister-in-law and her parents, my aunt and uncle, and my cousins, who attended.

My family, however, was more accepting than Lauren's. During our school break, she went back to her parents' house, and I called her using the phone number she had given me. A sweet voice answered the phone. "Hello," sung her mother.

"Hi, is Lauren there?"

"Who, may I ask, is calling?" Her mother's voice suddenly sounded formal.

I had a bad feeling. "Sara. From school."

"Don't ever call here again!" Her mother screamed at the top of her lungs. I heard the phone slam down, but it must have missed the receiver because it slammed again. She banged it so hard that I wondered if she had broken the phone. This was the end of me and Lauren.

A couple of years after Lauren, I began dating my first girlfriend. It took that long because I didn't know anyone who was gay—or who admitted that they were. In those days, a lot of the LGBTQ+ community was still in the closet. The internet was just beginning to make its way for mainstream use.

I leafed through the phone book, looking for the word *gay*. As luck would have it, I found the number and address of a LGBTQ+ bookstore. The building was pink, and it had a rainbow flag in the window. I was filled with curiosity. I walked around the store mesmerized by all the books—and the masculine woman, who had a shaved head and tattoos, working the cash register with a Mona Lisa smile on her face. The message I took from her was that she was totally comfortable in her skin.

On a bulletin board near the register hung a flyer for a weekly LGBTQ+ support group held in the bookstore. I decided to go. Men and women, young and old, single and in heterosexual marriages, sat in chairs forming a circle. There were tears, hugs, laughter, and fear as each took a turn to tell their story.

When it was my turn, I choked. "I'm just checking things out," I told them. Was I supposed to label myself with a letter? I thought that I must be the Q, if the Q stood for *questioning*.

A young woman in her midtwenties with bright-green eyes looked at me inquisitively. Angela had strawberry blond hair, a few freckles, and a pretty smile. If I met her on the street, I would not have guessed she was interested in women. Perhaps high school homecoming queen, which I later found out she was. Of course, now I know stereotypes are nonsense, but at the time I was ignorant and confused.

We chatted for a while at the end of the support group, and our conversation flowed. "Let's get together for a drink on Friday," Angela suggested.

I nodded with a slight smile, but inside, I was doing backflips.

I counted down the minutes until Friday. Finally, it had arrived.

Angela laughed and smiled often as we sat across each other at a table in an Indian restaurant. She was friendly, outgoing, and kind. Her long, thick hair looked straight out of a shampoo commercial. Her bubbly personality softened me, as I was generally skeptical of new people. During our date, I learned that she came from a tight-knit family. She had graduated from college, and she was a banking professional who was respected by her colleagues. She appeared safe, and in no time our date had progressed into a committed relationship.

We had been dating for a year when I asked her if we should move in together. "We are always sleeping at each other's places anyway, and we could save money on rent if we shared a place. What do you think?" Except for our family members and friends in the LGBTQ+ community, we told people we were just friends, roommates. We went on vacations with a same-sex male couple, and the four of us appeared as if we were two straight couples. If I was invited to a wedding or a work event, I typically brought a male friend as my date.

Angela came from a close family who reminded me of the 1950s ideal: family dinners, house decorations for every holiday, game nights, and her nephew's soccer games. Her parents—the captain of the football team and a striking cheerleader—were high school sweethearts. They had been married for thirty-five years and were the idyllic marriage that people admired.

I spent holidays with her family, who supported our relationship. I avoided my own family. My mom had developed a drinking problem several years before I met Angela, and talking to her as she slurred her words grated me. The contrast of being part of Angela's normal family provoked grief about my own upbringing. When we traveled to her parents' home for a weekend visit, I would wake up soaked in sweat from nightmares and sometimes hyperventilating. Angela would wrap her arms around me as I would try to regulate my breathing. Neither of us had the awareness to understand that something was wrong with me.

Gradually, Angela took on the role of caregiver instead of partner. She would regularly reassure me that she loved me even when I didn't want a gentle voice telling me I was loved. It didn't feel right. I felt pathetic and vulnerable. I wanted to feel strong. I had to feel strong. I had lived on my own since the age of fifteen and learned to rely on myself for survival after growing up with absent parents.

One day, Angela got down on one knee in our living room and asked, "Will you marry me?" She was holding a platinum band circled with diamonds. She even called my mom and my brother to get their permission first, which they gave her. I was twenty-four and way too immature to address my personal problems or to even be honest with my coworkers that I was attracted to women. I never wore the ring and sabotaged the relationship by working excessively and getting my graduate degree at night. I locked myself in our home office and locked her out of my inner world.

I moved on to the next long-term relationship, and then the next. My standards were rigid. My partners had to be educated, professional, attractive, healthy, and from upstanding families. No substance abuse. No drama. I liked things neat and tidy.

Between long-term relationships, I went on dates with men and women but often didn't make it past the second date. One of these second dates, with a medical student, ended particularly badly. We were watching a movie on my couch and she scooted up next to me.

I stiffened. She got closer and wanted to cuddle. She tried to rest her head on my shoulder. I stood up and said in an even and serious tone, "I don't want to cuddle, but I do want you to leave."

"You aren't nice," she said emotionally, with wide eyes.

"I know and never claimed to be. And I'm not a good person either. You are nice and will be better off with someone good. Please leave." She stood there shocked but didn't leave, perhaps wanting to talk, which I was not going to do. "Please leave. Now," I reiterated, calm and emotionless, walking toward my door to open it and shoo her out.

She scurried out with tears in her eyes. Dates with men were easier because they didn't push me for emotional connection. We could just hang out.

My coming out was a gradual process. The fear of rejection, or worse, was scary. My career was such an important part of my identity. Who would I become if I lost my job because of my sexual orientation?

Ultimately, I accepted that I felt stronger intimate and emotional connections with women, and I resolved to quit hiding who I was.

In my late twenties, I came out to my close straight friends and then my colleagues. Most of them shrugged it off. It was as if I had told them that I preferred chocolate ice cream over vanilla.

There were two exceptions, a friend and a coworker, who pretty much said the same thing: "What if you go to hell?"

This pissed me off. I didn't need anyone burdening me with their belief systems or judging how I should live my personal life. Did they assume that I had not done substantial soul-searching? Had they bothered do any soul-searching themselves, or did they just believe what they were told by some authority figure?

This fueled me to get involved with LGBTQ+ causes, putting me face-to-face with some vitriol, which increased my anger so much so that it buried the shame of being different. Or as adversaries would say, "evil," "disgusting," or "unnatural." I started by canvassing door-to-door to get signatures on a petition to change the state law so that no one could be fired from their job because of their sexual orientation.

Then, I got involved with the Human Rights Campaign, and I ultimately ended up on the LA chapter steering committee for the annual Human Rights Campaign Gala.

Later, Elizabeth and I would have such a good time attending those events and hearing speakers like Kamala Harris, Rob Reiner, Shonda Rhimes, Mariah Carey, and Joe Biden. While I volunteered with the Human Rights Campaign, I was able to visit the White House and lobby Congress for equal rights.

I began being categorized as liberal. Some used that term with contempt, even though I had been affiliated with both political parties before registering as an independent. Not being tied to a political party allowed my natural mistrust some space while I attempted to look at each candidate with an open mind. When same-sex marriage finally felt within arm's reach, I stepped up my involvement. I did a fellowship on President Obama's reelection campaign, as many of us believed he would play a key role in making same-sex marriage legal during his administration.

I teared up as I watched President Barack Obama and First Lady Michelle Obama dance together at his inaugural gala. This was a couple I looked up to. It wasn't until same-sex marriage became federal law that my anger dissolved enough that I could deal with the shame and pain underneath it and ultimately appreciate my sexual orientation.

In my early thirties, I was single again despite three long-term relationships. My hope of getting married was fading, and I was nursing my first real heartbreak after my failed relationship with Iris.

Iris captivated me from the moment I first met her at a friend's party. I turned my head to the right and there she was: wavy blond hair and a sculpted heart-shaped face. Like a magnet, I was pulled over to her, and I introduced myself. This was an uncharacteristically bold move for me. But it worked. I jotted down a note to self to be more straightforward in the future.

Iris told me that she had graduated from New York University with degrees in both environmental science and film. Check—she met my education requirement. She was a photographer, too. *An artist and a scientist. How cool.* She also shared her parents had been married for almost thirty years. Another check mark for Iris.

We hit it off right away; we had real potential. Such sudden and strong emotions were foreign to me, as I generally took my time feeling out anyone who was interested in me. Typically, I would hang out with any potential love interest as friends first. This way, I would be on alert for any red flags that might present themselves: drinking too much, not having a stable job, any issues with exes or family conflicts, etc.

But this wasn't the case with Iris. I jumped in headfirst, and I wrote her a poem about passing through golden gates.

From the get-go, our relationship was intense and dramatic. In order to tone it down, I did what I could to please her. When someone I briefly dated sauntered up to me at a party to say hello, Iris looked jealous, and I immediately cut off the conversation. When she complained that I traveled too much for work, I started taking her on some of my work trips. When she nagged about me hanging out with my friends too much, I merged our groups of friends. When she got mad that I was on work calls too late one evening, she threw my phone out the window of the Manhattan high-rise where I lived. This one got a reaction out of me. I looked down at the pieces of my broken phone and shrieked, "That could have hurt someone!" I seriously considered ending our relationship right then and there. This was a burning red flag that our relationship was not healthy. Instead, I walked out of my apartment and several blocks to the cell phone store to buy a new phone, which gave me time to cool off.

She always knew how press my buttons, and during one of our snowboarding trips, she asked why I was so absorbed in my work.

"I like my job." I shrugged.

"I think it's a way of pushing me away."

She was right, of course. But I said nothing.

"You keep me at arm's length."

"Can't we just enjoy snowboarding?" I asked her, trying to shift the conversation back to the sport. She got mad, and I got defensive. She grew more upset, and so, I tried to change the subject again. "Let's go to the fondue restaurant for dinner tonight," I offered. This was the most expensive restaurant in town, but trying to buy my way out of our conflicts wouldn't solve them.

Despite our conflicts, I desperately wanted for our relationship to work. But it only lasted a year.

The end came when Iris was accepted into two PhD programs, one in microbiology at Columbia University in New York, where we both lived, and one at the University of Michigan in Ann Arbor. She chose the program in Michigan, which meant either a six-year long-distance relationship or me moving to join her, which neither of us was ready for.

While I was hopeful that we would overcome our frequent arguments, the physical separation in a long-distance relationship was another story. I needed her near me. And while I pushed those I loved away when they got too close, when they got too far, it made me anxious and activated my fear of being abandoned.

As the date of her move to Michigan approached, I panicked. I was worried and wired. My heart would begin pounding, and my breathing became fast. I had trouble falling asleep, and once I did, I would sometimes wake up because of a nightmare. *Didn't she understand that I wasn't cut out for a long-distance relationship?* True to form, I ended our relationship rather than having to endure living in separate states.

Maybe a partner was just not in the cards for me. I swore off relationships and gave up dating for the next few years, but I hadn't come to terms with the possibility of not having kids. As I embarked on my thirties, with stability and financial security, I figured I would have a child on my own one day.

12

As I sat across from Janis, she held my timeline in her hands as if it were a cheat sheet. During the last several sessions, I'd given her an overview of each of the events that I had written down. I was basically briefing her on my life story as she took notes. In this session, we were at the finish line, discussing the last memory on my timeline.

So far this trauma work isn't so bad, I thought, not realizing we hadn't started the real work yet. We generally spent about eighty percent of each session going over my past, and the other twenty percent going over my present.

There were three themes that Janis and I discussed when we were going over the present: how terrible I felt for leaving Elizabeth, how haunted I felt for having feelings for Claire, and how badly I wanted to have a child.

After we finished going over the facts from the last memory, she shifted her approach and took me back to my early childhood, asking questions that were much deeper than anything she had asked me before. Frankly, it felt like she was gunning me down with this new line of questioning. How did you feel? What do you notice in your body as you recall that? Is there another time you felt that way? Did anyone comfort you after that happened?

I looked over at her office door several times and thought about bolting, but I stuck with it. I limped out of there exhausted.

After my session with Janis, I headed to the local nail salon for a pedicure to decompress.

I was greeted warmly by Jae, the nail technician, his perfectly manicured hands waving at me. "How are you today, Sara?"

I didn't even know he knew my name. I generally preferred to be anonymous, but I appreciated his warmth after the long hour I had with Janis.

I said hello to Jae and picked out a nail polish. I took a seat in the oversized maroon massage chair. As my feet settled in the warm water, I glanced at all the different colors of nail polish on the wall. There were more colors than a sixty-four pack of Crayola crayons. This thought warped me back into another time, and the room went out of focus.

My mind was no longer in the nail salon. I felt like I was standing behind my five-year-old self. The scene was so vivid that I could practically touch it.

I watched as this younger version of myself sat in a tiny, dark-blue plastic chair in her first kindergarten classroom. She was cleaning out her pencil box at the end of the school day. In it, there were large, thick crayons, which I liked to organize by the colors of the rainbow. There was also a large, thick red pencil, a fat eraser, some little yellow plastic scissors, and a bottle of Elmer's glue. I looked intently at the teacher as she released all the students from class, but her face was a blur.

I observed as my five-year-old self walked home from school and settled in her room. There was a giant E.T. doll, a twin bed with a pink blanket, a little table with two chairs, and Raggedy Ann and Andy dolls. I poured all of them a pretend cup of tea and gave them each a cookie.

I heard my mom calling my name.

"I'm coming."

I hurried into the living room, where my older brother was standing. He looked so young with his chubby cheeks and the faint freckles that were scattered across his nose.

My mom kneeled between us. "How do you feel about moving to California?" Images of the beach and Disneyland danced in my mind's eye.

"Yes!" I said. My brother was silent, apparently taking his time to consider her question. For me, it was exciting to go to a new place. I looked carefully at my mom for reassurance, and I noticed that her eyes were red and puffy. She looked exhausted.

It didn't occur to me then that we were running away from my biological father, Sam. When I was born, he was married to another woman. He and my mom had been having an affair and continued to do so on-and-off for years, even though he was married and would continue to be until the day he died.

I had only met my father a few times, and my memories of him were scarce. I knew he had a son and daughter, both several years older than me, and that he owned a successful small business and invested in real estate. My mom never said a negative thing about him, but she did break down in tears over him too many times to count, which is why I was glad he was out of our lives.

In 1982, when I was five, we moved to California so my mother could have a fresh start away from Sam. After loading the car with all the things we could fit into it, we took off on our cross-country adventure from Missouri to California. The trip was fun. We stopped at parks along the way and ate peanut butter and jelly sandwiches on picnic benches. Periodically, my mom would pull off on the side of the road to sleep.

"Sara?" I heard Jae call my name. "Sara," Jae said again, as he tapped my leg. It was time to pull my feet out of the water so he could paint my toenails. I felt a bit disoriented as I floated back in time again.

We had arrived in San Diego, and I was watching myself in a different kindergarten classroom at a Catholic school. My brother and I walked proudly to school in our uniforms: a plaid skirt, white blouse, and black-and-white saddle shoes for me, and navy dress pants and a white button-up shirt for my brother.

My mom had gotten a job waiting tables during the overnight shift at a diner called Rutherfords, and she volunteered in the school's library to cover our tuition at our Catholic school.

These were good times, and we were together a lot. My mom worked while we were sleeping, and she was home when we were home. We'd go out to get ice cream, and we'd save the pink plastic spoons. We had few household items, so the disposable spoons became part of our utensils along with some sporks from KFC. My bed consisted of blankets on the floor, and my brother and I unfolded and turned a futon chair on its side to create a wall between us when we went to sleep.

We were three peas in a pod. Weekends included all-day trips to the beach, where we played in the sand and used our bodies to surf the waves. We made bonfires in the evening, accompanied by music from someone's radio or people at the beach jamming on guitars and bongos. The air was filled with happiness.

"How does this look?" asked Jae.

"Good," I mumbled, disoriented, barely registering his words. He motioned me toward the drying machines.

Meanwhile, my past was yanking me out of the salon again.

One day, after I arrived home from kindergarten, my mom said a guest would be coming over for dinner. That night, a quiet, tall man with shaggy eyebrows and dark hair walked into our house carrying Happy Meals from McDonald's.

"This is Earl," my mom announced.

My brother and I started to play wrestle. I fell and split open the skin above my right eye on the corner of the coffee table. My eye stung from the blood that was dripping down into it. Earl applied bandages to the broken skin, and I felt happy that he was my mother's friend.

We moved into Earl's mobile home weeks later.

My mom made the move seem like a dream. "Sara, there is a community pool," she said, knowing I loved being in the water.

I was happy to see that the trailer was bright and clean with its own tidy yard. It was better than what I expected. Most of the people who lived around us were older and quiet, which was another plus.

The front door was on the side of the trailer with a few stairs that led up to it. It opened into the kitchen, and at opposite ends of the trailer were the living room and dining room with thin brown carpeting and two bedrooms, one for my mom and Earl, and the other for my brother. My mom set up a twin bed for me in the family room, and I kept my toys behind the little bar area, where I would crawl to play with them.

Shortly after we moved in, my mom declared that she was going to marry Earl.

I was shocked. Even though I was only six, I knew this was her third marriage, and we hardly knew this guy. I didn't like the changes I saw in her, either. My mom was absent when Earl was around, her attention always on him.

She tried to push me to embrace him, to call him Dad. "No. He isn't my dad." I asserted myself, and there was nothing she could do to convince me to call him anything other than Earl.

While I resented how she had become absorbed in her marriage, her new role as a stay-at-home mom had its perks. I would smell chocolate chip cookies baking in the oven when I walked through the door, and I watched as her garden came to life.

But my mom did not seem like herself. She didn't light up as much or laugh as much. A few years into their marriage, my mom and Earl developed a drug problem. They would take a razor blade and make little rows of snow-colored powder that would then magically disappear into a straw. My mom's eyes would go blank as she buzzed around the house cleaning, and Earl's tongue would involuntarily move in his mouth. Some nights, they didn't sleep at all.

As their drug habit worsened, other addicts began to hang out around our place. On Halloween, when I was ten, my mom, high, said to me, "Be careful sweetheart, Joe said he wants to kill you and use you as a human sacrifice for God." Her friends already creeped me out, but Joe was downright scary. School became my refuge, and I dreaded summer and holiday breaks.

Things continued to get bizarre. When we were driving, my mom would ask me if the car behind ours was following us. When I turned to look from the passenger seat, I saw an old lady driving a sedan. She also thought that the FBI was bugging our phone. I later learned that my mom and Earl were hooked on meth. The paranoia was a side effect of the drug.

I felt the nail dryer turn off, and I raced out of the door of the salon. I had enough sense not to drive, so I walked around the neighborhood trying to get my head screwed back on. But my mind kept going backward, and I wondered if what I was experiencing was what it felt like to be on drugs.

Ultimately, my mom kicked her addiction to meth, but Earl did not. After nine years together, and a few separations in between, she hit her breaking point. They divorced in 1992, when I was fourteen.

My mom told me that no dad is better than a bad dad. This was confusing. Earl was emotionally absent, but he wasn't a bad guy. In all their time together, he never missed a day of work at the Wonder Bread plant, he never yelled, and we had a ritual of baking pineapple upside-down cakes together. Maybe she was referring to his drug habit, which was fair, but did that make him bad? Both of their drug habits seemed to stem from either trying to escape reality or from trying to enhance reality, depending on the day. We moved back to Missouri, to the rural Ozarks region, and I haven't been in contact with Earl since.

I returned to the present as this thought thread ended. Things were a little fuzzy, as if I had just woken up from a dream. I turned my head from side to side, and I reconnected with the bustling neighborhood around me.

This was only the beginning. My past would continue to mingle with my present.

13

Even on a chill Sunday, I continued to have more intruding memories while I was sitting on a concrete slab in Gas Works Park. I was there enjoying the cherry blossoms that made the scene look like a vibrant painting. The flowers reminded me of my mom, and her love of nature. And now, most reminders of my mom seemed to transport me back in time.

My mother moved in with Teddy after divorcing Earl. She left me to live on my own at fifteen.

One night, while my mom was waiting tables at Thunder Mountain, a restaurant nestled at the end of a lake road that overlooked evergreens and deep-blue water, she walked up to a table to serve a man and his wife. My mom and the blue-eyed man locked eyes as he ordered a Southern Comfort to the disapproval of his wife. Like his drink, their marriage was on the rocks. The couple was living in separate homes, but they were attempting to take a family vacation.

My mom and the man at the table couldn't unlock eyes from each other. It was love at first sight, according to them. As she walked out the door at the end of her shift, he stood there waiting to talk to her. He had a huge smile on his face, and my mom's heart skipped a beat. From that point on, they were inseparable. Teddy filed for divorce immediately after meeting my mom, and she moved into his place within weeks. They were like two teenagers in love, and would continue to be for the next twenty years until he passed away from cancer.

I was on my own in our one-bedroom cottage, about a five-minute drive from my high school and a ten-minute drive from Teddy's condo. The peace and quiet of having the place to myself was relaxing.

Teddy was an alcoholic, and my mom developed a drinking problem as well after meeting him.

Every time I went to visit them, there was a party was going on, their friends coming and going through their revolving front door. She would be soused, her eyes glossy and blissful. Teddy would greet me, excitedly, like a golden retriever. He was the happiest alcoholic I've ever met. She knew if I lived with them, I would cramp their lifestyle, and I knew they would cramp mine.

I did fine on my own. My mom paid the monthly three-hundred-dollar rent, and I covered my expenses by working after school. I quit the basketball and volleyball team at school to pick up more hours to help my financial situation, and to buy a car. During this time, I also set off on the path of becoming a juvenile delinquent. I began to develop a bad attitude, and I started to skip my classes.

The only class I didn't skip was French. It was taught by a glamorous French lady who spoke elegantly, as if we were all in a Monet painting together. She was twenty-three and had long hair and a stylish wardrobe. She was different from the other teachers. One day, after class, she rested her hand gently on my arm and said, "My dear, travel through books." I don't even know what I asked her that warranted this response, but her response was worth remembering.

She had lived in Paris and seemed wealthy. Why had this young woman moved to my poor, rural town to teach? There was a rumor that she was dating my algebra teacher. All my classmates tried to figure her out, too, and we discussed this at our lockers.

The other reason I didn't skip French was because of Aliyah, a dark-haired girl who sat next me. I hadn't explored my sexuality yet, but looking back on this, I definitely had a crush on her.

One day, she looked at me, stressed. "I think I failed our quiz."

Why was this such a big deal to her? We had quizzes all the time. I felt a sudden urge to wrap an arm around her and comfort her. "Maybe you did better on it than you think. Either way, one bad quiz shouldn't affect your grade," I suggested.

She looked like she was going to cry. "I have to get an A in this class."

For the rest of the class, I half listened to what our lovely French teacher said in order to hatch a plan to remedy the situation. *I'm going to fix this for her*, I thought. This was only the first audacious act I would go on to do for a woman.

The stack of French quizzes sat in plain sight on the corner of the teacher's desk. The bell rang, and we all rushed out of the class. During lunch hour, I made my move. I hoped that the classroom would be empty and the door unlocked. And it was.

I crept in with the drumming of my heartbeat in my ears, and I rummaged through the stack of quizzes and found Aliyah's. I went through her answers and erased the ones that were wrong and circled the correct answers. I also glanced through some of the other students' quizzes, especially the ones I worried were struggling, and I fixed some of their answers, too.

After my mission was complete, I found Aliyah in the cafeteria, and I pulled her into a corner. "I fixed your quiz," I said to her, expecting her to throw her arms around me and thank me. But she looked at me with wide eyes instead.

Later that day, an announcement came over the loud speaker. "Sara Church. You are needed in the principal's office."

Crap!

Aliyah had ratted me out. This started my downward trajectory with the school's administration, and the first of a string of school suspensions. I was plastered with the *bad kid* label, even though I was an honor roll student. The label got to me because I had already been wondering if I was bad. Why would my mother and father bail on me if I wasn't bad? I started to skip classes more often and checked out of learning. What was the point of school? It wasn't paying my bills.

As the chip on my shoulder grew, the shell around my heart thickened.

Although I had been labeled *bad*, it did not free me from trying to be good. It did the opposite—it fueled a desire to prove that I was *good*. For now, bad or good, I just needed to set the labels aside and get through high school. At least I didn't have to worry about my mom. Teddy could look after her.

All I needed to do was to complete enough homework to get by, get to work on time, and keep the house clean. Everything else was gravy.

One day, when I came home from school, I found my mom sitting at my kitchen table. She and Teddy had an argument that day.

"It's over," she sobbed.

"It will be okay," I reassured her, giving her a hug while I looked over her shoulder at the clock. I needed to get to work.

My mom was back at his house by the time I got home from work. I was glad the drama was over. My home was quiet, and I was ready to fall into bed and crash after a long day.

The place where I worked for most of high school was an expansive Marriott resort. In addition to the hotel rooms and the cottages, it had a golf course, a spa, a sports complex, a marina, an arcade, multiple gift shops, and a conference center. The tourists drove around the compound in golf carts wearing salmon-colored shorts, golf shirts, and sunglasses.

Every summer, about one hundred college interns who were studying hospitality and tourism management came in from all over the world to work on the resort. The lake was filled with boats. Some were towing water-skiers, while others were carrying people to a cove so they could tie their boats together and party.

I worked in the Black Bear Lodge, a three-tiered restaurant with a bar at the top. There was a smoking section down one flight of the stairs, and the main floor was down a larger flight of stairs, with water views from the wide windows. On our busiest days of the year, like the Fourth of July, a thousand people would eat there, and we would set up a buffet.

I started out bussing tables, working as fast as I could to keep up with the herd of eaters. The white ceramic dishes banged around in my dark-brown bus tub as I carried it through the double doors of the kitchen before setting it down in the stainless steel dishwashing area. Occasionally, the teenage boy who did the dishes would glance up at me. His job was the only job in the restaurant worse than mine.

Unlike school, I had goals at work, and within a few months, I advanced to food carrier. My beeper went off when someone's order was ready. On a stand that looked like a luggage rack, I would set down a big oval brown tray. I would then load the plates and the condiments on it. I added stainless steel covers over the plates, bent my knees so I could place the tray on my shoulder, and I was off to the table. This was a promotion. Not only did it pay an additional twenty-five cents an hour, but it also meant that management thought me worthy of interacting with the guests at their tables.

After a few more months, the assistant manager pulled me aside and asked if I would like to serve the tables. "Yes sir!" I responded. Although the hourly pay was lower, the tips were significantly more than what a food runner made. The only problem was that I was a minor, and in the state of Missouri I was not allowed to carry the drinks to the table until my eighteenth birthday, so the bartender would have to do it.

I greeted folks warmly but efficiently. I studied the specials carefully every day, and I practiced describing them without an Ozarks Missouri accent. People eat with a *fork* not a *fark*. I made a point to be polite when taking orders. I said, *Yes, Sir*, and *Yes, Ma'am*. When they were finished, I'd ask if I could please take their plates, and when they nodded, I said *thank you*, and *have a great evening*. All of this paid off in higher tips.

I bussed my own tables if a bus person wasn't around to do it, so that I could decrease the time before another table would be seated in my section. At the end of my shift, I happily gave a portion of my tips to the bartenders, the bus people, the food runners, and the hostess. It was important to have them on my side.

If someone, other than the bartenders, needed one of their shifts covered, they usually came to me first. It didn't matter if it meant working seven in the morning to ten at night or if I got blisters on my toes and heels or if it was back-to-back doubles. The work invigorated me, and my pockets were lined with cash. My work addiction hatched at the Marriott.

With more money than other high school kids, I felt confident and accomplished. I even opened a savings account and put twenty to fifty dollars in it per week, depending on how good my tips were. I bought a car—a forest-green Dodge Shadow that I washed every week. I bought nice clothes, a gold necklace, and gifts for my friends. Hard work and independence as ideals were chiseled into my brain—Howard Roark happened to be my favorite book character at that time.

After two years of living on my own and working at the Marriott, I decided to drop out of school, and, instead of completing my senior year in high school, I went to the University of Wisconsin–Stout, in Menomonie, to study hospitality management. My plan was to open my own restaurant (this was the only industry I had experience in). The buzz of working in a fast-paced environment intoxicated me. Phoebe, my favorite intern who I drank too much with on the night of my seventeenth birthday, planted the seed of higher education in my head. She told me that I should go to her to college in Wisconsin.

The idea settled in. I called the admissions office to find out how I could get into the university that Phoebe went to. The angel on the other end of the phone would end up holding my hand throughout the process. I pretty much harassed the admissions department with weekly phone calls. Cold turkey, I took my GED and SATs then submitted my application materials—and it worked. I couldn't believe that I actually got into college.

I invited my mom to take the long drive to Wisconsin with me. She was excited to come along. I hand washed and waxed my car, and I drove to Teddy's to pick her up. My car gleamed in the early morning light as I pulled up to his condo.

I had called her before I left my house and asked her to wait outside. Going into Teddy's place could result in a long, cheerful conversation with him that I didn't have the time or energy for. When I got to the condo, she was nowhere in sight. *Why wasn't she waiting outside?* We had a long drive ahead of us, from Missouri to Menomonie in northern Wisconsin.

Within a few minutes, I saw her walking down the stairs wearing a hot pink sparkly headband. I sighed with relief.

Cheerily, she hopped into the passenger seat. She smelled like booze from the night before.

"How exciting! A road trip to college. I am so proud of my baby."

Baby, huh, I thought. *I'm the adult in this duo.*

After driving for a few hours, I felt tired. "Mom, are you ready to drive?" I asked.

"No," she said as looked out the window. "I'm enjoying the view. There is so much to see in our beautiful country." Her voice cracked a little—she always wiped tears from her eyes anytime someone sang "The Star-Spangled Banner." I kept my annoyance bottled up. I decided to change the subject, a pattern I had established in my early childhood. When I got angry at her for her negligence, she would look confused or sad, and then I would feel terrible and comfort her. Showing my distress wasn't worth the effort.

As I continued to drive, I reflected on our relationship, what it was like growing up with her. I had often had to ask her multiple times if she had remembered to pay the bills.

"Remind me of your flight details?" I asked her. She would fly back to Missouri after dropping me off.

"It's around six tonight, out of Milwaukee."

"Milwaukee!" I snapped. I tried to take a deep breath to calm myself. "That's four hours away from campus."

"From Menomonee Falls?"

"No. My university is in Menomonie. On the other side of the state." I kept my voice as steady as I could. This detour would mean that I would arrive very late for a check-in meeting at the admissions office. Though I was used to her mishaps, and this wasn't a surprise, I was boiling inside.

I dropped her off at the airport around lunchtime. She threw her arms around me and shed more tears. She was proud that I was going to college. The minute she exited the car, I stepped on the gas pedal and a peace settled over me. I was now an adult, and this was my new life. In that moment, I cleaved my childhood. I locked it in a safe, and I exiled it into my unconscious. *The past is over—the future is my oyster.*

When I pulled up to the university solo to start my new life, I felt alone and poor. The parking lot was full of cars, trucks, vans, and even U-Hauls. In the brick dorm building, parents and students carried in suitcases, popcorn machines, microwaves, and futons. Whole families were here to drop off kids at school. And here I was, carrying two suitcases of neatly packed clothes, a radio, and nine hundred bucks I had saved from my job.

I decided to replace these feelings with my new sense of independence. I thrived. I didn't skip any classes, and I worked hard at my campus catering job and in the business school office. But I also played hard. I went out every Thursday, Friday, and Saturday night with friends.

Despite working two jobs and having a robust social life, I managed my time and did fairly well in my classes. The trick was to not waste time. I didn't sleep past eight in the morning, I didn't watch TV, and I stay focused in my classes to reduce study time.

And just after my twenty-first birthday, I graduated. My mom, Teddy, my brother, two of my aunts, and my grandmother came to my graduation to celebrate with me. We only received four tickets, so I had to get two extra. Quite an improvement from arriving at college alone. I thought I was moving up in the world. But twenty years later, I realized I was on my own again.

14

"How do these memories make you feel?" Janis asked me at our next session.

I looked at her, puzzled. "I don't know." They were unwelcomed and annoying interruptions in my day.

"It's common to have a lot of memories in between counseling sessions. We are unpacking a lot. Today, let's go back to your first memory." I wanted to go back out of her office door. Why didn't she just cut to the chase and take me to the big stuff like the missing memory of the shooting? I mustered up my resolve and complied with her direction.

I lowered my eyes, and an image of me lying on the couch while my mom changed my diaper emerged. My mom looked at me and said, "Go get Mommy a diaper." If I was in diapers and could walk and do this simple task, I might have been two or so.

I leaped off the couch and ran down the carpeted hallway to my bedroom door. A diaper bag hung from the door, and I pulled out a diaper and ran it back to my mom.

"Good girl," she said. "You are such a big girl."

"Describe how your body is feeling, now that this memory has popped up," said Janis.

"I feel relaxed, but I got distracted calculating how old I was in the memory. It doesn't seem possible for me to have memories that young." Janis didn't respond and nudged me with her eyes to continue. "I don't think I feel anything about it. But there was pride in my accomplishment, getting my own diaper. I guess I do feel something. Why?"

"It is possible to have memories from when you're a toddler. It sounds like it is a good memory."

"Yeah."

"Any idea why?"

"It felt good knowing I got the job done."

"Not like being triggered. What do you feel when you're triggered?" she pressed.

"My body tenses up, my vision is weird, and my heart races. Maybe I feel angry. Or I just shut down. Go emotionally offline," I responded, trying to understand Janis's line of questioning.

"Give me an example of when this is likely to happen."

"Sure, when I walk into a messy house. It makes me feel irritated, and I want to leave. Piles of clothes, dirty dishes, the smell of cigarette smoke or stale alcohol make my skin crawl. It's a relief to get back to my clean house where everything has its place. No mess. No clutter."

"You are a person who needs order," Janis stated the obvious.

"Yes." I was embarrassed to admit to her that I color code my clothes. And my desk at work has a pencil holder, a note pad, and a docking station. That's it. If the environment is too messy, I have trouble concentrating. I can get by, but it drains my energy.

"It's chaos that makes me most uncomfortable. In 2010, I went to Times Square on New Year's Eve. My friend was dating a sergeant from the NYPD, and he was able to get us a good spot to watch the ball drop. We were in a roped-off area, not in the pack of spectators, about ten feet away from the crowd. The whole scene had too much commotion, and it was like I was in a lucid dream, watching it happen not being a part of it."

"This description sounds like you were experiencing derealization, a form of disassociation," said Janis. "One of your first steps toward recovery is to get in touch with your body and feel the sensations as they're happening, as uncomfortable as they may be. This is something you will need to work on. Once you get this down, we can then work on how to self-regulate emotions."

"Got it. Step one is to feel my emotions and bodily sensations." There was a certain ease and comfort in being disconnected from my emotions; giving this up would be a big deal.

Janis guided me so I could gain experience by regularly pausing when I shared something. "What are you feeling right now in your body, physically and emotionally?" she would ask.

"Heaviness in my body. Glass shards in my heart. Butterflies in my stomach. Waves of fear across my chest." Very gradually, identifying feelings and body sensations helped me connect to my emotions. I didn't have any problem being attuned at work, but with loved ones, it was another story. Usually, I detached and numbed out with those closest to me.

That night, I got to work on my new assignment. I started with a simple but effective practice of labeling my inner world. *What am I going to eat for dinner?* I'd label that as "thinking." *Why hasn't my mom called me? Is she okay?* That one was a "worry."

I took my time to notice how my body felt. Did my chest feel tight? Did my stomach feel acidic? Were my shoulders hunched? My fists clenched?

Labeling took a ton of self-discipline. I could only do it for a few minutes at a time, but it brought self-awareness and presence—a step toward emotional maturity, which I defined for myself as being in touch with my emotions and able to manage and express them in a constructive way. I noticed if I was having productive or counterproductive thoughts, and I had the realization that my thoughts needed to be managed before they ended up managing me.

Although the labeling was a useful tool, it peeled away more layers of my internal onion, and it uncovered more buried turmoil that I hadn't realized was there. My inner world felt out of control, and out of control was the worst and scariest feeling in the world for someone like me. I was working on being whole on the inside, so I couldn't find any shortcuts. A Robert Frost quote came to mind at just the right time: "The only way out is through."

15

I had been meeting with Janis for several months now, and things had only grown more intense with each passing week. My memories went from drips to a moving sprinkler that was soaking me with questions.

Unpleasant feelings popped up all over the place, even during heartwarming moments. I would see a happy family—parents and their joyful kids—and I would feel upset, their laughter piercing my heart with the pain of what I didn't have. I tried to offset all of this by imagining different possibilities for my future.

I decided that it was a perfect day to walk on the Burke-Gilman trail that went around Lake Union. The kind of leisurely Saturday that was ideal for daydreaming. The deep blue water sparkled from the reflection of the sun, and the seaplanes and sailboats made the scene even more magical.

As I walked, I glanced across to the other side of the lake and saw the tangle of office buildings; one of them was the one I worked in. The mountains in the distance contrasted with the urban setting of Seattle and made for an awesome view.

I imagined what it would be like to stroll here with Claire. In this fantasy, we have two to four kids, at least one girl and at least one boy. Two of each would be nice. Friday night is game night. Our house is located on Lake Washington, a hub for our friends and family to hang out. It has a wooden dock with a boat and kayaks, and a semicircle of Adirondack chairs facing the water, wrapped around a fire pit, perfect for s'mores. And of course, vacations to beaches and to fascinating cities all over the world. We both progress in our careers to afford all of this, and we become more involved in our local community. We celebrate our fiftieth anniversary party on an island with family and friends, and we hold hands as our kids and grandkids toast in our honor.

The fantasies flow. And not just in a fairytale way. It would even be nice to bicker with her about whose turn it was to take out the garbage or nag her to not forget to put the toothpaste cap back on. What reasonable person wants their toothpaste to dry up, making it hard to squeeze out of the tube? That was how far I let this fantasy reach before pulling myself back to reality.

The world had been overwhelming my senses lately, and I felt raw in it. So many things annoyed me: noise, quiet, talking to my mom on the phone, not talking to my mom. I used to spring out of bed to go to work, and now I dragged myself up. I used to have padding around my belly, and now I was skinny. Too skinny.

Was it worth it to revisit the past? I made a commitment to myself to heal. I had already broken the commitment of marriage. I had to keep this one.

I tried every trick in the book to race through the healing process, but nothing fixed me. I tried to exercise more, set goals, see my friends, listen to inspirational podcasts, read psychology books, but nothing worked. There was a tornado whirling inside me that wouldn't let up.

Man, I missed my old life and my old self, the oblivious self—the self that could shut out her emotions, ignore the turmoil within, and go about her business.

But I was intent on not letting this get to me. I would not give up. I decided to try a new approach. I was going to make myself look better on the outside, which was something I hadn't tried yet. I got a haircut and a facial, and I hired Miranda, a personal shopper, to help me. Miranda had me try on a bunch of clothes. She would enter the dressing room with a stack of shoe boxes that went higher than her head. And although this would thrill so many people, it didn't thrill me. The rumbling inside me came with me into the dressing room. I was stuck. I was totally stuck.

Stop being a self-absorbed privileged brat, I criticized myself. *Look at where you're at today! At fifteen, you were stealing money.*

This happened when I worked in a mom-and-pop restaurant in high school, before I got my job at the Marriott. The restaurant got less busy as the months ticked by. One payday, I looked in the slot for my paycheck, but it wasn't there. I figured they'd just forgotten.

A week went by and, still, no paycheck. I kept working. Thankfully, I was making tips. Another week went by and no check. Other employees were concerned the business was going to have to close. I asked the cook if we were getting our paychecks.

"Don't count on it," he grumbled.

I was stressed. I needed that money. And I was mad that they had taken advantage of us. There was no way I was going to let them take advantage of me.

One night, after the restaurant closed, I climbed in through a window that was unlocked when my shift ended, and I went to the cash register and took the amount of money they owed me, and a soda for my trouble. It hadn't occurred to me that it was wrong to break into the restaurant.

By crossing the line, I had compromised my values. Even at age fifteen, I was aware this didn't feel right. And it made it easier for me to take another step in the wrong direction, and I went even further. I shoplifted a Ralph Lauren shirt by rationalizing that, unlike other teenagers, there was nobody else to take me shopping to get clothes and other goods and my ratty clothes were a source of insecurity.

It felt wrong. I had to make a choice about the kind of person I wanted to be. I decided to never steal anything again. And I didn't. I made a decision to do something, and I did it.

Remembering this gave me the motivation to keep plugging away with Janis.

I purchased several of the items that Miranda brought into my dressing room, which caused a dent in my bank account but not in my healing. It felt good to be put together on the outside, though.

16

I heard the loud boom of an explosion. I looked out the window. The city was under attack by a foreign military. Seattle was filled with sounds of bombs detonating, sirens, and people screaming. I got in my car to escape, and I found myself downtown. I saw another bomb drop in the distance. A mushroom cloud appeared in its wake. People were frantically running in the streets with nowhere to go. A smoky stench of dead bodies filled the air. Ash, blood, and debris everywhere. A toddler looked up at me, and I scooped her up and started sprinting, but there was nowhere to go.

Another nightmare.

I woke up soaked in sweat, and I got out of bed and changed into dry clothes. These middle-of-the-night wardrobe changes were becoming commonplace.

Too rattled to go back to sleep, I looked up dream interpretation online to try to make sense of it. Perhaps the bombs exploding represented all the emotions blowing up inside me. The mushroom cloud represented the cloud that loomed over me making people run away from me. The foreign enemy was the part of me that I didn't yet understand. There was nowhere to run because I couldn't escape my feelings. Or, maybe the dream was simply telling me that I had blown up my marriage and hurt someone I loved.

A couple of nights later, I had another dream. This time I was in a small, blue bedroom with my mother and a man. I was a little girl, and I was hiding behind a chair. He was holding a gun. He looked me in the eye and pointed the barrel at me.

"No!" I tried to scream, but the word wouldn't come out.

He shot me in the chest. My ghost floated out of my chest and saw my lifeless body sprawled out on the carpet and my ghost tried to scream at him. "How could you! How could you!" But he couldn't hear me. I woke up in my bed shivering from the sweat, but I was glad to realize it was only a dream. I thought back to my last session with Janis.

Janis had glanced at my timeline and said, "Okay. It's Christmas Eve. Your mom and your stepfather are using crystal meth in their bedroom."

I dove back into the memory, and I watched it, numb, as if it hadn't happened in my life.

I saw a nine-year-old girl in her house. The dark carpet, the unfinished drywall, and the urine around the toilet. My stomach churned. I watched as my younger self put herself to bed, and I saw her wake up in the morning to run over to the Christmas tree. She grabbed a present and shook it. She was curious about what was inside. She went to find her mom to get permission to open the presents.

But her mom wasn't in the kitchen. The girl went down the hall to her mother's bedroom; the door was partially opened. Her mom and Earl were in the same place as they had been the previous night. They were wearing the same clothes, smoking rock.

"Can I open presents?" the girl asked. Her mom looked at her with vacant eyes, got up, and closed and locked the door, shutting her out. The girl laid down outside of the door, crying.

Looking at her crumpled on the floor, I felt my stomach burn and a stabbing pain behind my ribs. I knew things would get worse for the girl before they would get better.

With one foot in the past, and one foot in the present, I described to Janis what I was seeing.

She told me to escort the child out of that drug-infested house and asked me to take her to a safe place. As usual, I gave Janis the benefit of the doubt and did as she requested.

I held the girl's hand, and I took her on an imaginary walk along one of my favorite beaches in Malibu.

Janis then asked me to take the girl to my current house, so I could show her how I lived. I took her on a tour through the house where Elizabeth and I lived before we filed for divorce.

I walked her up to the front door of the three-story house. We entered through the clean entryway and stopped at the bench to take off our shoes. My road bike was leaning against the wall.

I walked the wide-eyed girl upstairs. She looked around the house and went over to my fridge, and I opened it for her. The fridge was full with food: milk, eggs, fruits, vegetables, and some leftover takeout. There was not a dish in the sink. The white walls and the light wood floors gave the house a bright, airy feeling. In the dining room sat a midcentury oval marble dining table, with six walnut chairs around it. Along the wall that divided the dining room from the living room were shelves filled with books and two healthy houseplants.

We went up the stairs toward the master bedroom. My bed was made. The clothes in my closet were clean and organized into categories and by color. The girl looked pleased. I felt a hint of pride.

Janis spoke as if she was talking to the nine-year-old instead of me. "You don't need to worry. Everything will be all right."

Then, she spoke directly to me. "When we are wounded as children"—she paused—"children who are unhealed still live within us. These inner children have defense mechanisms, like anger, for instance, that were created to protect them at the time that they were hurt. Defense mechanisms are a healthy and adaptive response to toxic stress in our environment."

This all sounded strange. She tried to explain again. "The problem is these defense mechanisms remain after they are no longer necessary. They have been protecting you so long, even though you are now a capable adult who can take care of yourself. It's important that the unhealed, hurt children in you trust that you will take care of them so your defense mechanisms can be released. The first step is to befriend all of your wounded inner children. Then you can establish self-leadership."

I found this hard to believe. My psyche had wounded children of different ages running amock with their accompanying defense mechanisms in tow and all I needed to do was to do convince them all, that is, myself, that I have control of the wheel? This seemed too weird and too simplistic to be true. It sounded farfetched.

In all fairness to Janis, it had occurred to me that in many of my recent nightmares, children of various ages were involved.

17

Despite being buried in healing work and dealing with the divorce paperwork and the accompanying guilt, which I had not befriended, I was keeping my head above water at work. Somehow, neither my boss nor my friends seemed to notice I was off. It helped to have the appearance of normalcy. Only the few people who knew me best could tell I was struggling. *Were other people struggling too and pretending everything was peachy?*

Janis thought I was stable enough to go through the eye of the storm, but she held eye contact with me and reiterated her earlier warning that my symptoms could worsen before getting better. She wanted me to do a kind of memory reprocessing work called EMDR. While I was impatient to resolve any lingering trauma and move on from being in therapy, I was hesitant about going any deeper into my past. I had a sense that my life was being held together by a thread, and I was fearful that the thread would break.

EMDR is a therapeutic technique that enables a person to focus briefly on the traumatic memory while simultaneously experiencing bilateral stimulation. The technique reduces the intensity of the memory, though no one has been able to explain to me why in a way that I understand.

"I think it will help you," Janis said. "It's an effective technique for processing past traumatic events so that they lose impact on your present life."

I crossed my hands over my chest.

She reassured me that this method was backed by research and had been proven to have good outcomes. She added that she would refer me to some studies if that would help.

This was acceptable for me. As long as there was data to back this approach up and not much to lose, I was in.

"It has even shown solid results for people with complex PTSD," Janis added.

Complex PTSD! Back up. Complex PTSD? This did not sound good.

"I understand your confusion. You have complex post-traumatic stress disorder. It's a type of PTSD that results from chronic stress associated with abuse, neglect, or abandonment. Think of it as layers of traumatic events over time rather than just one traumatic event, like an assault."

Death by a thousand cuts, I thought.

However, I did not fully trust this PTSD diagnosis, yet another label in my life, until many months later after I got a second opinion to confirm this diagnosis from another PhD who specialized in trauma. Mistrust is common for many who have experienced trauma. Why should anyone who was hurt or let down by the people who were supposed to take care of them trust easily?

I gave Janis my consent to do EMDR and left her office with my head spinning. This sent me on another reading spree to understand the diagnosis. My take from the information I consumed was that I could have developed PTSD as a result of the shooting I had possibly witnessed: a one-time terrifying or life-threatening event. But it also could have originated from the ongoing stress from growing up in an unstable and unpredictable home environment. By not having a parent or caregiver who was able to meet my needs with enough consistency, I had developed an insecure attachment to caregivers. This insecure attachment style often follows people into adult relationships with romantic partners, as the insecure person, not feeling safe, sabotages their relationships. I chalked this up to why my issues only showed up in intimate relationships. Certainly, I had a history of panicking when I got too close to someone or becoming unsettled when they were too far away. Another description I spotted that fit me was relational attachment trauma. The labels didn't matter much to me as long as I healed myself. Generally, Janis referred to me as someone with PTSD instead of c-PTSD to keep it simple. The information I read also gave me evidence that the issues were all solvable and that "earned secure attachment" is attainable, which left me optimistic I could be just as healthy in a relationship as a person who didn't have childhood trauma.

What I connected with most was reading about others' personal experiences. One account that struck a deep chord with me was "A Day With: Complex PTSD" (much appreciation to the author, who generously allowed me to include an excerpt):

My life is woven together by threads of trauma. None are explosive enough to solely cause post-traumatic stress disorder (PTSD). But it's the impact of dozens of smaller traumas combined that landed me in a psychologist's office with a complex PTSD diagnosis.

That was five years ago. Back when the stress of a turbulent divorce and serious health problems left me incapable of using my normal coping skills. I couldn't work harder or achieve more to prove my worth because I was too sick to work at all. I went to therapy to "fix" my problems and get over childhood pain, but instead, it unleashed a monster that swallowed me whole. For six months, CPTSD left me curled up on the bathroom floor, shaking and sobbing, reliving my past traumas. There was no past or present, just the cold hard bathroom tile, feeling incapable of stopping the tsunami of memories and sensations.

After reading personal stories like this one and scientific data about post-traumatic stress disorder for a week, I was armed with questions for my next meeting with Janis.

"What happens to a kid's brain because of trauma?" I asked her.

She explained as if I was in a lecture hall that trauma can alter the structure and the functioning of the brain, especially a child's developing brain and their nervous system. She added that studies have shown significant neurobiological changes in three areas of the brain: the amygdala, the hippocampus, and the prefrontal cortex. "The limbic system, which is key in our emotional and behavioral responses, is altered."

Is she saying I have brain damage?

She took a stab at applying it to me in layman's terms. "Your brain and nervous system are wired to be hypervigilant of, and overly sensitive to, things that remind you of or expose you to the risk of rejection, abandonment, or loss of someone you love. You will likely react with a flight, fight, or freeze response, as this reaction is the rational response to your background."

Feeling deflated, I said, "So, in a nutshell, you're saying I have to change my brain?" Another option that popped into my mind was to avoid any triggers, but the cost would be that I would not be able to form or sustain an intimate relationship. A life of flying solo didn't sound bad, but that was my fear of commitment talking. Over the months ahead, I would seriously consider remaining single for the rest of my life to bypass this condition.

Learning all this brain stuff from Janis was mind-blowing. The emoticon of the exploding head summed it up. How in the hell was I supposed to repair my brain and nervous system?

Oddly, as I sat quietly across from Janis, a little voice inside of me responded, *You're going to get through it the same way you got through other hard things. Grind through it one day at a time.*

Janis sensed the questions running through my mind and said exactly what I needed to hear. "Your brain can positively change both structurally and functionally throughout your life in response to your new experiences. This is called neuroplasticity. People develop new neural networks and pathways, but it takes time. I believe that your PTSD is not only manageable, but it is curable."

I wanted my dream—a happy family. I was taking steps forward on having kids, and I wasn't comfortable with moving forward with these plans until I resolved my issues.

"Well, I have to fix this. When can we get started with EMDR, and how long will it take?"

Janis raised her eyebrows. "Progress can be made even in just a few sessions. But we need to process several events from your past. Healing is a journey. Be patient with yourself."

Patient was the last thing I wanted to be. "Okay. I'm game. Let's do it." Janis pulled out two little paddles that creeped me out. They were shaped like the rocks you would collect for skipping on a lake. I had to hold one in each hand while she guided me through a memory recall and processing practice. The left one would quietly vibrate, and then the right one would vibrate.

I felt spooked, and I shifted awkwardly on the couch. *Could my life get any weirder?*

Janis decided to push me into an ice-cold pool. "Let's start with the memory of your mom going to prison. That seemed to be the most pivotal turning point in your life."

When I was nine, my mother went to prison for fraud. She had previously worked as a secretary at a used-car dealership in 1980. At the time, her boss was having the mechanic set odometers back. Later, she'd been accused of being complicit with their scheme.

"Sounds good," I said, as I masked my reluctance and skepticism.

As I felt the paddles vibrate from left to right, I went back to 1986. This memory was graphic.

I was standing on the sidewalk in front of my school looking out at the parking lot, waiting for my mom to come around the corner and pick me up. She was planning to take me to the mall after school to get my ears pierced.

Where was she? I glanced around the school parking lot, and I saw all the other kids had been picked up. Buses were returning to school from their routes.

Finally, a tan pickup truck came around the corner. Earl's truck. He was at the wheel.

My heart dropped in disappointment.

"Where's Mom?" I asked him.

"Get in," he said, while staring at the road. We drove silently in a direction that was neither toward home nor the mall.

Where were we going?

A few minutes later, we pulled into the parking lot of a police station.

"Your mom has been arrested," he finally revealed.

I couldn't believe my ears. My mother was not a criminal. He must have been mistaken.

He spoke again, "The police are saying her boss was setting back odometers at the car lot she used to work at. They are saying she knew this was going on. They are saying it is a felony charge." I felt like I was going to vomit but remained composed. What if my mom was going to be locked up for years? I had no idea when I would see her again.

Janis had once told me that traumatic memories can get stored in the body and show up physically. This could explain why my stomach hurt so much when a loved one was late getting home. Although I was in the memory, I was also in the present and aware of Janis and the buzzing paddles. This was a new experience—to be consciously present in two time points at once.

While my legs wobbled, I entered the concrete jailhouse and walked across the blandly tiled floor. They looked like hospital floors. Earl walked next to me, stoically.

My stomach dropped as I saw a Plexiglas wall with a line of brown plastic chairs facing it. The chairs looked similar to the chairs at school, but larger. On the wall hung a black corded phone. I took a seat in the third chair and Earl stood behind me. My mom was wearing a jail-issued beige jumper. Her face was as serious as if she had just received a cancer diagnosis. I couldn't even hug her.

I lifted the phone to my ear.

"Sara," she said, her voice shaking. "I got pulled over for speeding and the officer took me in because there is a warrant out for my arrest in St. Louis. They are going to transfer me to Missouri tomorrow." A few years ago we had moved to California from Missouri, and I was terrified my mom would be taken to another state, where I couldn't visit her.

I broke into tears, and I slapped the palms of my hands on the clear barrier trying to get to her. She pressed both of her palms on the Plexiglas. Her eyes looked helpless. I slapped harder against the barrier and yelled, "Mom!" Immediately, the guard came over and told Earl to remove me from the premises.

I opened my eyes to see Janis sitting in front of me. My eyes were dry.

"How do you feel?" Janis asked.

"Fine. Calm," I said, not understanding that I was cut off from my emotions.

Janis was prepared to go into battle. "When did your childhood end?"

The words immediately jumped out of my mouth. "It ended when my mother went to prison." That's when the pain and the tears that were buried below my memory broke through. My insides throbbed in agony, and Janis just sat with me as I rode through the emotional waves and memories.

My life changed irrevocably then. In many ways, I went from being a child to self-sufficient adult. My stepfather, Earl, seemed to disappear. He went to work and retreated to the bedroom when he came home. Maybe his drug problem resulted from my mom going to prison.

My brother, a teenager at the time, stayed out at night. And my mom's family lived in another state. It was just me and my dog most of the time.

If I wanted laundry done, I did it. If I wanted to eat, I prepared my food.

"Earl, we are running out of food." I told him one day.

Earl worked at the Wonder Bread factory and would bring boxes of Twinkies and Ding Dongs home. Now, even those were running low. He reached into his pocket and handed me a twenty-dollar bill and motioned me to his truck. His radio filled the silence with oldies, the voices of Ray Charles and Elvis making their way out of the speakers.

He dropped me off in front of the grocery store.

As I pushed my cart through the aisles, my chin the height of the handlebars, I read the price tags and the food labels. It was important to calculate the cost per ounce so I could save a dime here and there. A jar of spaghetti sauce that was priced fifty cents less than the others mattered because I could buy an extra can of soup with those savings. The soup meant lunch.

While I analyzed the cereal boxes, I glanced up to see a woman staring at me with what I perceived to be a judgmental look. Defiance rose in my belly. I stood taller. What is her problem? I'm just shopping like everyone else.

After that day, Earl dropped me off at the grocery store every Saturday afternoon and waited outside in his truck for me until I was done.

He didn't get involved in my daily life or with my school, but I didn't need him to. Every weekday, I got myself dressed, made my bed, ate breakfast, and walked to school. After school, I did my homework. My performance skyrocketed. I was racking up accolades: first place in the science fair and the math olympics; I became a crossing guard, and passed the Presidential Fitness Test; I got straight As, and I was even voted on the student council. This must be when striving became my coping mechanism.

I glanced back up at Janis. She was quietly sitting there, present in my messiness, and that was all she needed to do. Simultaneously, I was nine years old and I was forty. My worlds were overlapping, yet still split into two, past and present. They were both hard to be in.

I pitched my head forward, spent from the EMDR, shaking off the past.

"Good work, Sara," said Janis. "Let me know if this becomes too much. Remember, symptoms may get worse, and more things may come up between our sessions as we continue to do deep reprocessing. It's normal."

Janis always acted as if I was normal. This was not my definition of normal.

18

I headed to Irwin's, one of my favorite coffee shops in Seattle. It had distressed oak tables with mismatched chairs and Scrabble and chess boards. The fragrance of the coffee beans and the pastries in the room were revitalizing. I sprawled out on one of the couches and read the news. I didn't have a care in the world.

That is, until my eyes landed on an article about prison reform. My insides were on fire as I read about the racial and socioeconomic inequities around incarceration. My heart started beating faster as my mind raced back to my mother's time in prison and her return home about six months later. The person who returned home was not my mom. She was a shell of a person with all the light drained from her eyes. I wrestled tooth and nail to get the images that had come up during my last EMDR session out of my mind.

I counted. Three, six, nine, twelve, fifteen, eighteen. I kept going until I was grounded. Grounding was a technique that Janis taught me. Previously, I tried her suggestions of noticing the pressure of my feet on the ground or finding five different items of the same color, but counting worked best for me. This empowered me. I could regain control over reliving my past.

Still, having the past barge into my consciousness had become disruptive, exhausting, and it fogged my ability to enjoy my day to day. Worse, it made my identity feel shaky, as I had always known myself to be a together person. It was becoming challenging to experience the beauty around me: a warm cup of coffee, a view of sailboats floating in the water, a person holding the door open for me, an interesting article about health care a colleague had emailed, or a phone call from a longtime friend.

I made a mental note to put extra effort into staying in the present so I could enjoy all the tiny wonders and notice the little moments that make up most of our lives.

And here and there, a funny thing started to happen. I started to notice the flowers in greater detail than before. The vibrant colors and intricate patterns painted on their petals. Rainbows began to show up more frequently, or I had become more aware to catch sight of them when Seattle's drizzle and sunshine coexisted. A whole string of magic moments beaded together, and they would later become an important indicator of my well-being and happiness. The more of these beads that I had in a row, the more amazing my experience of life was.

19

Claire and I chatted at the end of our class one day, and as we talked, there was this magnetic energy pulling us together. I fought off the ever-present urge to keep distance between me and her, and I opened up.

I shared about what I was working through in therapy, and about the girl who was shot, who was perhaps my friend, when I was an adolescent. Claire listened with compassion in her eyes, and, surprisingly, she didn't look at me like I was damaged.

In return, she opened up about the soul-searching she had been doing about her sexual orientation. Her life was overwhelming, too.

As we walked out of Hugo House, I noticed an old white car parked outside with a man sitting in the driver's seat. I froze. My surroundings began to swirl and everything start to look blurry. *The scenes of a white four-door sedan clicked through my mind. The windows of the car were rolled down. There was asphalt. The parking lot at Alberto's. The place where Gloria lost her life.* The images didn't tell me a cohesive story, they didn't even make sense, but they terrified me.

It disturbed me that these images hadn't come up in the controlled environment of Janis's office. They were happening on an ordinary evening. I can't remember if I said good-bye to Claire nor do I know if I walked slowly or briskly to my car. And I was too overwhelmed to use the grounding techniques. I had just enough awareness and impulse control to keep from slamming the gas pedal and peeling off. I sat frozen in the driver's seat.

Over and over, these images ticked through my mind. This flash-back threw me into a tailspin. I put my forehead in my hands. I wanted to scream "Stop!" but nothing came out.

I got ahold of myself and got home safely. I received a text from Claire checking to make sure I was okay. She must have noticed that my eyes were bugging out as I left Hugo House.

These were not the first images to come up for me from that fateful day. In therapy, I had reached the point where Janis and I were working through the shooting. I still had no idea if I had been there or not. Or if Gloria, the girl who was shot, was my friend or just a neighbor.

What I did know was that I recently had images barge into my consciousness: a parking lot, a white car, a bus, a dirty ditch, dusty pink high-top sneakers, Earl's dented truck all flickered through my mind like an old-school photo projector. These images were on a reel that repeated over and over again. A carousel of fragments.

Although these images kept replaying themselves, round and round, my memories revealed little. Even when I re-read the letters that my mother had brought me, my being emptied to nothingness.

I decided to book a last-minute trip to California for the weekend. I was sick of therapy. Sick of thinking about my past. Sick of being bro-ken. I wanted to move on with my life and take the bull by the horns to get to the bottom of this.

I stayed the night at a friend's house when I arrived, and I woke up early the next morning and hopped into my rental car, a black Range Rover. I splurged on the car because driving it gave me a fake sense of power, especially when I was feeling powerless. I headed straight to the restaurant where the shooting took place, desperate to put the puzzle together.

The drive took a couple hours. I head south, down Interstate 5, to Oceanside, the town where the shooting happened. I didn't need to look at the GPS map. My arms automatically steered me off the right exit and down a winding road. I drove past fields, a neighborhood, and a park. I approached a stoplight, and when I looked up at the street sign, I saw I was at the intersection of Redondo Drive and North River Road.

Time seemed to be moving in slow motion. My foot tapped on the gas when I saw the traffic light change from red to green. I glanced ahead, and saw Alberto's, the Mexican restaurant where the shooting happened, on my right. On my immediate left, on the opposite corner of the restaurant, was a bus station. Behind it was a ditch that looked like a miniature dirt canyon. Almost three decades later, the restaurant and parking lot eerily matched the one in my memory. The scene looked like it had been preserved in a time capsule.

I wasn't sure how I had found this place without a GPS. I had only lived in this neighborhood for about six months, a few years before I was old enough to drive. I am the type of person who doesn't even remember the address where I lived five years ago. I get turned around going to University Village, a shopping area that I go to regularly and is a practically a straight line from my house.

I pulled into the parking lot of the restaurant and stepped out of the Range Rover. I hoped for a miracle. I was hoping that this place would bring me cohesive, connected memories and solve my interpersonal problems. But the same reel of pictures played in my mind—the parking lot, the white car, the bus going by, the dirty ditch, the dusty pink high-top sneakers, and Earl's dented truck. I felt surprisingly relaxed, perhaps I was detached, as I turned and looked toward the restaurant door behind me.

A story began to unfold in my mind's eye as a couple more images emerged in short fragments. Teenage girls walking out of the restaurant. People and cars in the parking lot. A city bus passing. A white car driving by with its window down. There is some commotion. A girl with dark hair and eyes falls to the ground. The ditch. A dusty hill that leads to my neighborhood. My high-top sneakers, the pink-and-white ones, are covered in dirt. Earl's truck arrives.

I took out my phone and snapped several pictures of the scene: the restaurant, the bus depot, the ditch, the parking lot. *Maybe looking at these later might help to release a clearer story.*

As I drove back toward the highway, I took a detour through this familiar neighborhood. It was where I lived when I was thirteen. The main road was lined with small houses. I took a left on a street with a cul-de-sac where simple ranch homes sat. I saw myself hanging out in the living room of one of the houses with a dark-haired girl my age.

My drive from Oceanside back to LA was silent. My heart was still, and the logical part of my brain was trying to solve a puzzle that had missing pieces. A few more memories came up about the neighborhood.

A circle of teenagers beating up another kid at the park near my house. And a fight between two girls my age, on the school playground, that everyone gathered around. A girl standing next to me said, "Look at all the rings she is wearing." Referring to one of the girls in the fight who had bulky metal rings on every one of her fingers. "The rings are so she can tear up the other girl's face." My stomach churned as the girl's cheek ripped open. I walked away.

Shame was the first emotion that broke through with these memories. Shame for doing nothing to intervene, just running away, as kids got hurt.

Over the next couple of years, this would be the best story that I was able to piece together: *If* I was there, I must have gone to Alberto's after school with girlfriends, one of them being Gloria. Once we finished eating, we headed out into the parking lot, where some young people were hanging out. We stopped to talk to another group of teenagers in the parking lot, as the road buzzed with cars and buses, when a car drove by with its windows down, and a gun was fired. People scrambled, and I must have run across the street, through the bus depot, and down the ditch toward my house. A stray bullet hit Gloria, which caused her to fall to the asphalt. My mom must have been at work, and my seventeen-year-old brother was out with his friends. I called Earl, even though he was separated from my mom and had not been living with us, and he came over to pick me up. Perhaps this event was a catalyst that helped bring Earl and my mom back together.

Shortly before my mom and Earl reconciled, my mom announced we were moving. We went to look at a new apartment a few miles away. My mom and I walked around the small, clean apartment. She smiled and said it was nice. I thought it seemed peaceful, too.

"They don't take dogs, sweetie. You are going to have to get rid of Mariah." Mariah was my dog, a black-and-white border collie. She was my best friend—more than a best friend, she was my family. I'd named her, I fed her, I slept with her, and I brushed her fur every day.

Resigned to my fate, I put an ad in the newspaper. A few days later, a couple with three young kids came to pick her up.

I watched with my face pressed against the glass as they drove off with my dog.

We never moved into that apartment, or any apartment for that matter. A month or so later, Earl picked us up, and we moved back into our old place. The place with a yard, where my dog, Mariah, used to live, too.

More emotions continued to break through the detachment. Sadness expanded in my chest until I had to hold tears back from seeping out of my eyes. My feelings started to poke through regularly until they flooded me. Janis wanted me to connect with my feelings, but we hadn't touched on how to regulate them, much less master them.

I didn't tell Janis that I was going to LA, because I thought she might talk me out of it. So at my next appointment, I confessed to her that I had traveled to the scene of the shooting. She didn't look upset. I recounted the whole trip to her while she patiently listened to every detail of my excursion.

Finally, I asked her what I been wondering for so long. "Janis, do you think I was there when Gloria was killed?"

How could I trust my brain, when it might have hidden, or even altered, memories about my past? If I didn't know that I'd lost important memories, how, then, do I know if I found them?

Janis did something she rarely did: she gave me her direct opinion. "Yes, in my professional opinion, I think you were there." She paused. "Traumatic events affect memory in one of three ways. One, the memory is burned into someone's mind, which then recalls a vivid experience with details, like your hands banging on the plexiglass when you saw your mother in jail. Two, the event is stored as fragments, with only a few pieces of information being recalled, and the other details are forgotten. Or three, the memory is blocked out, which is what I think happened in your case. Sometimes people recover these memories and sometimes they do not."

I looked at her skeptically as I chewed on this information.

She added, "And, even if you weren't there, you still lived in that neighborhood, and a horrific event like that could have been traumatic for you and any of the other kids in your neighborhood or school who knew Gloria. This is why I think it's important for counselors to be available for all students, especially after a big loss or disaster." Next, she revealed an insight. "People don't have to recover traumatic memories in order to heal traumatic events from their past."

Her last statement was music to my ears. "You're saying don't have to remember past events to repair any damage from them? My goal isn't to be in the past, it's to be healthy in my present life."

When our session ended, I thanked her for the information and for her opinion. The most important thing that I took away from the conversation was that I didn't have to spend so much energy trying to recall and analyze past tough events in order for me to get over any negative impact they caused. This made it okay for me to not know what happened. And it allowed me to reorient my focus toward the future. One where I was mentally healthy so I could have a family.

And when I was ready to, I let Gloria's death go, with a prayer for her and her family and with the hope that her soul was resting in peace. Ultimately, all of the flashbacks and images stopped.

20

One morning, I woke up tossing and turning at three. My mind was worrying about my future. I rolled out of bed and treaded down the stairs to the living room, where I turned on the TV, but this distraction didn't quiet my mind.

I needed silence. So I crossed my legs like a buddha statue on my new rigid, camel-colored leather sofa, and I closed my eyes. I began to meditate by focusing on my breathing.

My first experience with meditation had been ten years earlier. I had stumbled across an article about meditation that raved about the positive health benefits of this practice. The writer went on to share several studies, which included a study from Harvard where researchers found that meditation resulted in positive changes across the brain regions that helped with stress, memory, and empathy. I was curious, so I decided to copy the study's protocol.

For eight weeks, I meditated daily. Over the weeks, I noticed changes with my focus at work, and I started to reach for healthier food options. I began taking the stairs, instead of the elevator. Within a month, these positive changes happened automatically without me giving them a thought.

By the end of eight weeks, my pants fit better, and I was more connected to myself and the world around me. Things appeared more alive. The sound of birds chirping filled me with joy. The pleasant smell of the salty ocean air delighted me. A man petting his dog on the boardwalk warmed me.

I decided tonight was the night to get back on the horse and see if meditation would fix my limbic system and still my mind so I would be able to get back to sleep. But meditation wasn't helping me tonight. A hurricane of thoughts swarmed my mind and was accompanied by aches in my chest and discomfort in my legs. I took a deep breath and and tried to meditate again.

Determined to conquer meditation and my mind, I went back to surfing the web and typed in the words *silent meditation retreat*. I found one that would be starting in a few weeks at the Insight Meditation Society in Barre, Massachusetts. I checked my work calendar to make sure that I didn't have any major work events coming up. This ten-day silent retreat would be possible to pull off if my boss, the only person I answered to, approved my leave. *Could meditating ten hours a day screw my head back on straight?*

A few weeks later, I strolled through the Seattle airport with a tightly packed backpack and a winter coat in my arms. A few hours and a couple of glasses of airplane wine later, the plane landed in Boston.

I took an Uber to Insight Meditation Center, where I was dropped off with my backpack miles away from civilization. My mobile phone had a couple bars of service, so I could make a phone call if necessary. I craned my head up to look at the enormous red brick retreat center. It looked like an old mansion or an old boarding school. Four white Roman columns guarded the large front door.

I glanced at my phone once more before entering the building. At the front door, a sprightly, friendly middle-aged woman welcomed me.

"Welcome to IMS. Here is a bag for your phone and information about the retreat." She handed me a plastic Ziploc bag and a two-page handout.

I knew we were going to be silent for the ten days, but I didn't know they would confiscate my phone. My palms got clammy as I handed over my phone, my beloved companion. The woman took the plastic bag that held it and dropped it into a basket piled with other phones.

She then went through her spiel. "A bell will chime at five-thirty to begin the day." She pointed her pen toward my handout and gave me an overview of each bullet on the schedule:

5:30 a.m. wake up (and shower for me)

6 a.m. meditation

7 a.m. breakfast, eating meditation

8 a.m. meditation

9 a.m. chores

10 a.m. walking meditation

Break (nap for me)

11 a.m. meditation

12 p.m. lunch, eating meditation

1 p.m. meditation

2 p.m. walking meditation

3 p.m. yoga or meditation

Break (another nap for me)

5 p.m. meditation

6 p.m. dinner, eating meditation

7 p.m. lecture (from a monk)

7:30 p.m. meditation

9 p.m. bed

Then, she told me about my daily chore. "Your role will be to clean the bathroom."

My whole body tensed as I thought back to my childhood. I used to have to clean the disgusting messes in our bathrooms made by the addicts and the strays my mom and Earl brought in. There was always urine crystalized under the toilet seat, which made my gut wrench.

I asked her if there was any other job I could do, but she looked at me as if I had two heads. And I was off the grid without a mobile to call a taxi. This was my cue to accept that I would be cleaning the bathrooms for the next ten days. I remembered the Buddhist saying I had on my bulletin board in my office.

A man asked Gautama Buddha, "I want happiness."

Buddha said, "First remove 'I,' that's Ego,

then remove 'want,' that's Desire.

See, now you are left with only 'Happiness.'"

The woman continued with her orientation. "There are only a few rules. Follow the schedule and don't communicate in any form. No phone calls, no emails, no writing, no reading, no talking. Absolute silence."

I needed to do this. I needed to do something! My inner world was a mess, and I was unfulfilled.

And so, for the next ten days, I resigned myself to the rigors of the retreat, and I settled into hours of daily meditation. I felt safe being in this monastery-type setting, away from the world and away from my life. It was refreshing.

I scanned the dozens of faces of the other people who were attending this meditation retreat, and the diversity was remarkable. It appeared every age, race, and walk of life was here. We were all connected by being in this individual and shared experience.

The monks were fascinating. The two women, who were probably both in their fifties, had shaved heads and wore crimson-and-gold robes. They both looked regal as they gracefully entered the meditation hall, their heads high and their eyes gentle, ready for the first evening lecture.

Initially, I spent a lot of time trying to figure out how to comfortably sit on the meditation cushion. But within a few days, I had adjusted. I fell into the routine, but my mind continued to be restless.

I wonder how work is going? My rowdiest colleagues popped into my head. These were the outgoing, fun people you wanted at your party. I imagined them sitting here hour after hour, day after day, meditating. I almost laughed out loud when I pictured them cross-legged and silent in the meditation hall. My entire body jiggled as I suppressed the laughs.

It took forever for the lunch bell to chime.

In the cafeteria, we were all completely quiet. I watched a squirrel through the window stop to pick up an acorn. And for twenty minutes,

I watched it nibble through the acorn. In a silent retreat, this kind of thing was on par with a James Bond movie.

About a week in, my mind finally chilled and felt peace. There were periods of utter quiet in my head, empty of any thoughts. I remembered someone once telling me that the average person has three thousand thoughts per hour, and I had a few long stretches of no thoughts.

It's not like my distressing thoughts stopped following me altogether—they followed me like a shadow. As much time as I spent in peace, I also ruminated on why my past relationships flopped and what my feelings for Claire meant. But as consuming as these thoughts were, they were easier to deal with in the retreat center. It started to make sense to me why someone would choose to do this for months, even years. There was a serenity to this cocoon.

I waited for an epiphany, any insight that would make everything make sense and allow me to become whole. Or the key to unlock the door to a meaningful life.

When that didn't come, I decided I needed to build a relationship with my mind, I needed to get to know how it functions, so that I could become better acquainted with my thoughts and emotions. I began to experience what my meditation teachers spoke of: "Thoughts and feelings are like passing clouds in the sky. You are the sky. Then the clouds float away. Stay mindful and observe the thought or feeling. The awareness observing is your essence." The identification of the thought or the observation of the feeling provided me with the time and the space to figure out how I could better respond. This space was where I understood part of our power to create to be.

There was also a sense of accomplishment in knowing I could last meditating for ten days, multiple hours a day.

But the most important outcome, after the shock of learning I had PTSD, was that none of my thoughts were freaky. This was huge. Going into the retreat, I had no idea what I would find lurking in the depths of my being. I was afraid that bizarre thoughts or feelings would emerge while I was meditating. But only regular things, like relationships, work, and whether I should exercise more, came up. These thoughts didn't scare me. They made me feel like an ordinary person, which was exactly what I wanted to be.

However, I still had miles to go before I would be able to manage my mind, my emotions, and my behaviors. I needed to heal more, and weaving these mindfulness practices into my daily routine would accelerate my progress.

At the end of the retreat, once we got the green light to resume communication, the room boomed with noise. We buzzed around introducing ourselves and sharing the basics of our lives, like where are you from, or, is this your first retreat? At long last, our phones were in my field of vision. The woman who checked me in handed me back the plastic bag that contained my phone.

I turned it on and watched all the messages populate. It seemed like I had missed little at home, and at work my team did just fine in my absence. I made a mental note to disconnect from work more often. Overall, it was a wonderful and interesting experience. I was excited to get back to my life and move forward with these new mindfulness tools in my tool belt.

PART III

Most big transformations come about from the hundreds of tiny, almost imperceptible, steps we take along the way.
—Lori Gottlieb

21

The divorce process itself went relatively smoothly for me and Elizabeth. Although my heart hurt, we had been able to move through it amicably, negotiating the terms peacefully and equitably. Initially, I shut out the pain that surged through me, and I decided to focus on the logistics of the divorce. The most difficult decision we had to make was deciding who got Leo, our beagle. Elizabeth took Leo but agreed to let me visit him periodically at his daycare. It gave me some solace that she wouldn't be totally alone, but I missed him. And I missed her. And so many things about our life together.

We used an Excel spreadsheet to list our assets and divided everything by two. One of us would email the other with the spreadsheet attached like we were working on a project together. I had asked Elizabeth if she preferred to keep the house or to be cashed out for it. She decided to move out of the house, but she generously left me with more than half of the possessions in the house.

Elizabeth had been civil, reasonable, and kind throughout this tragedy, even as she said that she didn't know where the person she married had gone off to. I was emotionally disassociated when I walked out, but she didn't know that.

Back in the house, heavy hearted and lonely, I busied myself by unpacking my suitcases from the Airbnb where I had been staying and got to work organizing the household items that remained. I touched up the paint around the house, and I put a big plant where Leo's bed used to be because I would tear up every time I looked at that spot. Leo couldn't be replaced, but the plant added a touch of comfort. As serendipity would have it, a puppy was about to find its way to me.

One day, during a work meeting, I sat in the back with a colleague, who is a ray of light wherever she goes.

"Hey, Sara. Look at this," she said, showing me a picture on her phone. "My friend's dog had puppies yesterday. Aren't they the cutest! They all need homes."

I eyed the photo of the five adorable border collie–mix puppies. Two were black and white, another was brown and white, and the remaining two had marbled fur.

The black-and-white ones looked like my childhood dog, Mariah. "I want one!" I said, the words flying out of my mouth.

Within a couple days, I had submitted the application the owner had sent me. It was a long application, and the pressure of knowing she had other people interested in the puppies made me feel like I was applying to Harvard.

Why would she choose me? Why trust me to give the puppy a good home? I wondered. I was living alone in the city, in a house with a rooftop deck, not a backyard.

I brushed off the negative thoughts, and I let myself hope that she would accept me as a puppy owner. She did.

A couple of weeks later, I met the puppies. They were just learning to walk and would take a few steps before tipping over. The puppies would nuzzle up together and bump their heads into each other. They couldn't yet wrestle.

While I played with them, my problems seemed to melt away, and the cloud that I felt hovering over me lifted. They were all adorable. But one of the black-and-white ones—the first one to walk—snuggled up close to me, licking me, as his tail wagged in every direction. I cradled my future puppy in my hand, and I was filled with happiness.

As I prepared to welcome this new addition into my home, I was also welcoming a positive focus. My future seemed brighter. I signed up for puppy classes, and I refreshed on my puppy-caring knowledge: how to bring one home, how to train them, and how to socialize them.

Seven weeks later, Zac came home. He threw up on the seat of my car as we were driving home. He peed on my floor five minutes after we walked in. He cried throughout his first night. And he ran around cutely bumping into the walls and cabinets and chewing the corner of one of my stairs. Although chaotic, I loved chasing him around, paper towels in hand.

He loved to be held, and he attacked his squeak toys with gusto. He learned how to sit during his first puppy class. And by the time he was six months old, he could catch Frisbees. He seemed to drop more than he caught, but still, it was amazing that he caught as many as he did.

When I took him to his vet appointment, the vet said to me, "This is the most affectionate dog I have ever met," as Zac licked her arm. The first time Zac saw me sad, he ran up to me. He tried to jump on my lap, but he was too small and stumbled. Determined to heal my wounds, he followed me wherever I went. He whimpered when I got into the shower; even this quick separation from me was hard for him. When I emerged, I'd find him nestled into my pajamas on the bathroom floor.

We took care of each other and became inseparable; Zac was always in the same room as me. At least I formed a strong connection with my dog.

With Zac at my feet, I was ready to survey what items Elizabeth had taken, and what she had left. I also needed to make a list of what I would need to purchase. It was time to stop eating using plastic take-out spoons and forks. After researching flatware online for an hour, I ended up purchasing the exact silverware Elizabeth and I bought after we got married. Next, I purchased an Eames recliner much like the one we had in our living room, except this one was cream instead of black. I wanted to change things up to make them seem a little different, but I also wanted to keep things similar to remind me of the familiar and of Elizabeth. She had an eye for quality, and she scrutinized purchases carefully. I trusted her.

I decided to go to a shop to find furniture for the outdoor deck. This was much easier to choose. Unlike the silverware and indoor furniture, patio furniture didn't evoke memories of Elizabeth and me because we never got around to furnishing the deck.

"I'll take this whole patio set," I said, as I waved my hand in the direction of the display. The sales clerk's eyes questioned me. "The chairs, the couch, the throw pillows, the lights, I want everything." I settled for purchasing the already curated set because it was easier.

To make the house feel more like a home, I bought a couple more plants, and I placed an arrangement of flowers on the dining room table. The bookshelf was filled with books, and my teething puppy bounced around attacking all the new furniture like it was a bush in the wilderness.

When I finished arranging my new purchases and cleaning, I glanced around the house, not fully satisfied with the progress I had made. The house looked like I'd staged it. It was a little too perfect, too sparce, and too put together. And, still, the house looked . . . well, empty. It was so empty that it echoed.

But at least now things appeared better and shinier.

At work, thing looked promising, too. I got a promotion, which astounded me, given I was so worried that they could see through me and into my messy inner world. Recently, I had told my colleagues, people who I respect a great deal, about my divorce. I feared they would think less of me or not trust that I had it together enough to perform at work.

I also had an appointment coming up with Seattle Reproductive Medicine to put together a fertility plan.

But these external things coming together had tricked me into a false sense of confidence, like things were finally falling into place, and I could handle everything on my own. *I don't need anyone* had been my mantra, on and off, since I was child.

In preschool, my mom had to leave work in the middle of the day to pick me up from the office, after the school had called to tell her I was being ornery and obstinate and wouldn't conform to the rules. The teachers looked flustered as my mom told them that she would handle it. She looked amused as she took me out of school for the day.

Years later, she still had no control of me. When I was in fifth grade, she kicked me out of the house because I was arguing with her. She told me to pack a suitcase, and she handed me a quarter for the pay phone. "Call your father. Tell him to come get you."

The problem was that I had only met my father a couple of times. He lived in another state, and I didn't know his phone number. *Hmm,* I thought, *I could call 411 to try to look him up*? But that would cost me my quarter, and it was all I had.

I banged on our front door and yelled, "No, I won't call him. I'll live on the street!" And as I turned to walk down the driveway, my suitcase trailing behind me, my mom rushed out of the front door and told me to get back in the house.

This incident reiterated a belief system. I could only count on myself at the end of the day. But maybe now, I was making enough progress to jiggle this mindset away.

22

My relationship with Claire started on a hot summer day, after our writing class was completed. This intelligent woman had melted my heart into a puddle, albeit a puddle that rippled with fear.

I picked up the phone and dialed her number. My hands were trembling. Even a simple act like this required a level of vulnerability that I was still not ready for. On the second ring, I thought about hanging up, but she picked up, offering me a warm hello. After we bantered for a bit, we hatched a plan to meet at her house and then walk over to the park. I parked at the curb in front of her next-door neighbor's house, which I decided to adopt as *my spot* if I were to be invited back. Parking in the ample room in her large driveway would also have required too much vulnerability.

My anxiety allayed when I saw her approach me with a huge smile on her face. We strolled over to the park while we talked casually, although my chest was filled with butterflies as I rambled on about work.

There was a moment of silence. I was peering at my feet, and I inhaled a deep breath, trying to muster every ounce of courage inside me. And yet, I didn't know what to say.

She peered deeply into my eyes as she grinned, placing her hand over mine with a slight squeeze.

But I couldn't relax. My stomach was in knots—this was scary. I had been daydreaming about being with this woman, and here we were.

I admitted to her that I was raw, processing grief and guilt about my divorce. I was a mess, as I was knee-deep working through my PTSD. And I was overwhelmed trying to have a child. I wanted to give her all the disclaimers up front so she could run away, fast. I would have, in her shoes.

I hoped she wouldn't leave, but I would understand if that's what she decided to do.

But she didn't seem troubled by what I told her, and that afternoon, she took me into her arms and reassured me that she wanted to be with me.

As much as I wanted to believe her, and although I felt close to her, this closeness generated fear for me. I wanted to trust her, but I wasn't sure how to fight my internal impulse to be wary of intimacy. But the intense connection we had would continue to surge us forward.

A few weeks later, I felt at ease on one especially joyful summer day. We were lounging on the grass in a park near a lake watching Zac frolic around as his tail wagged. I wrapped my arms around Claire, and I ran my fingers through her hair. The scent of her shampoo floated through the air.

The birds were like our personal orchestra. The sunlight danced on the water, while the ducks and their ducklings glided along the surface. Children were laughing on the adjacent playground, and I was laughing, too. Claire made me laugh . . . a lot. Her humor was understated, but her expressions were animated.

Back at Claire's house, she seared salmon and prepared a green salad loaded with vegetables for us. I watched Zac run around her yard as I sipped a glass of wine, waiting for a meteor to crush me. This day had been too perfect.

Except, I was about to demolish our wonderful day. I dropped the meteor.

When we sat down to eat dinner, Claire told me that she would be leaving tomorrow for work and would return later that week.

My heart grew heavy. I felt my chest fill up with concrete. Whenever she was away, which was usually half the week or more, my nightmares would happen more frequently.

I tried to remain calm, reminding myself that she regularly checked in when she was away. She'd send me these stunning photos of the scenery, all of which I had saved in a folder on my phone. I knew that she always prioritized seeing me when she was able to.

Why was I even bugging out over this? I traveled for work regularly, too, and I enjoyed being autonomous and having time and space for myself. My self pep talk didn't work, and the alarm turned into numbness. I tried to cover it up by asking her nonchalantly if she was ready for her meeting the following day.

Detachment was my first line of defense. Generally, I grew as emotionally flat as a crepe in relationships when I was unsettled. But due to the work I was doing on myself, my first line of defense was becoming weak. Breaking down the defenses was an early sign of progress, but I didn't know this yet, and I didn't heed Janis's warnings that the healing process can make things messier. Overwhelmed, I moved from one defense to the next, meeting parts of myself that I didn't know or like. My next line of defense was to criticize, and my last line was to run away.

I would yell at myself when I created drama, which would work for about five seconds. And then I proceeded to push her further and further away. The pain in her kind eyes would break my heart. Shame filled me, but it still didn't stop me from harping on whatever I found to fight with her about. Something as minimal as her lunch bag having an image of a cat on it led to me questioning her if we were a good fit because I was a dog person and allergic to cats. *Man, I sucked.*

After I got ahold of myself, I attempted to repair things. I told her I was sorry, but that I had once read an article about how cats would eat their owner's corpses, but dogs wouldn't—this was hardly a good way to take accountability for my venomous words, let alone to apologize to her.

She greeted my apology with her mouth half opened. But her face quickly turned into a silly twist, and she said that she didn't think all cats would eat their owners. How would they do that anyway? This was a perfect example of her understated humor, but also of Claire's own avoidance of communicating her own feelings.

23

"What is verbal abuse?" I asked Janis during our next session. I was pretty sure I knew the answer to this, as I had done some reading on it after picking a fight with Claire. This was just my clunky way of opening the session.

Janis looked perplexed. "Verbal abuse is about controlling another person by using emotions and words. The behaviors can include things like name calling, lying, and isolating someone from their friends and family, blaming, stonewalling, bullying . . . Why do you ask?"

Why was she puzzled? Didn't she understand that I was a monster? Words are very serious weapons that carry the power to injure a person at the deepest level.

I didn't want to sugarcoat my bad behaviors; I had to be honest with myself if I wanted to do better. "I do some of the stuff you mentioned. Like criticize, pick fights, and get hot and cold."

"Is your intention to control Claire?"

Her question stumped me.

"No, not at all," I said, as a rogue tear escaped my eye. "Well, maybe. Yes. The thing is, I don't want to control her. At all. I just want to feel like I have control over my own life." Since Claire and I had started dating, the chaos inside me had intensified, and it was terrifying to not feel control over my emotions. My army of defenses came ready for battle.

Janis looked at me with a concerned look in her eyes.

"A relationship is a dynamic between two people," Janis said, not giving me the belief that I could own or solve these relationship problems on my own. She seemed to be hinting at a previous lecture she had given me about the Trauma Reenactment Triangle. The Trauma Triangle consists of three things: a victim, a rescuer, and a perpetrator. Each of these roles have a motive and a payoff. She suggested that we had become stuck in a pattern where I was usually the victim or perpetrator, and Claire was usually the rescuer—fixing, pleasing, and appeasing me. Claire was the good guy, while I was the bad guy.

Don't be so nice! I wanted to snap at her when she played Miss Fixit. But at the same time, I wanted to tell her that if she wanted to help me, and help us, get through this, I needed her to sit with me and stay emotionally present, as sucky as it was to be with my hellhole of emotions.

Claire's response to our conflicts, or rather, my intimacy triggers, was to tell me to reach out to her when I was in a better place. She would then proceed to fill up her calendar. She was a fortress of steel when she was hurt, and I tried to ram my way through her walls, lashing out with angry emails or texts. This never got me anywhere. I would only feel more guilt for not treating her right.

After a few sleepless nights, an elevated pulse, and crippling anxiety, I would inevitably pull myself together, and I'd reach out to her to set up a time to talk, though I was exhausted from fighting with my demons.

She was open to this, and she would suggest a time for us to meet.

During these conversations, Claire was always loving and sincere. She wanted to find solutions that would make our relationship work and compromises to my complaints, which were mostly about my fears around rejection or abandonment. Of course, I didn't open up to tell her that at the heart of it I was afraid that I would lose her. That she would leave me.

At the time, it didn't occur to me that Claire wasn't sharing many of her feelings and she wasn't asking me for anything. As giving as she was, I walked away from these conversations feeling needy, damaged, and, ultimately, more insecure. I wanted to help her, too. My contributions seemed to be few and far between. I did find her a cat sitter, though. I wanted to strive for an egalitarian relationship, one where we would each look out for each other and our relationship.

But I was too busy pushing and pulling to try to find a tolerable level of closeness.

Janis was the first to articulate the obvious. "Are you afraid Claire is going to leave you and not be there for you like your parents?"

I nodded. I'd come far enough to make the connection that Claire's distancing behaviors reminded me of the times I was on my own as a kid, physically and emotionally.

"Being triggered is no excuse to be a self-absorbed," I said, frustrated. I despised excuses and sought total accountability. I had been working on myself all year, but all that seemed to come out of it was emotional flooding that was drowning me and this new relationship. I needed Janis to give me the magic pill—fast—to help me regulate all these emotions.

"That extends to yourself as well. Have you ever thought about being kinder to yourself as a way to help you be kinder to Claire?" she asked me. Janis had preached to me many times that how kind you are toward yourself translates to how kind you are with others.

Absolutely not. That didn't make any sense. I needed to push myself more. I didn't need to baby myself.

24

On my drive home from Janis's office, I listened to a podcast to get my mind off things. It was a physics discussion that went over my head, but my ears perked up when the speaker said that *energy cannot be created or destroyed, it can only change form.* The Laws of Thermodynamics made me realize that I had been spreading bad energy lately, which was the polar opposite of the person I wanted to be. But I didn't yet know how to be the person I wanted to be. Somehow Claire was able to remain positive despite the negative juju I had been emitting.

Did Claire have the energy to be there for me and deal with me and my PTSD? Would she have the bandwidth to be there for me if I got pregnant?

Our relationship had been an unexpected and disruptive event in her life, in part, because I was the first woman she had dated. *She has issues, too, right? Her past relationships failed, too.* That is, in addition to the issues I created. That was a question for her to figure out, or to avoid and not figure out.

Claire seemed to have her own fears and protective layers as well, which kept a barrier between us. In certain ways, she seemed to like her life as tightly controlled as I did. I had the clean house; she had a precise military schedule. I had the emotional outbursts, and she put walls up when her emotions overwhelmed her. Even though I was intensely frustrated and spiraling with Claire, I looked toward my future and still saw children in it, with or without a partner. This mattered most to me, and I stayed the course on my plans to have kids.

When I was thirty-two, a few years before I met Elizabeth, I had been single for a few of years. While I wished I had a partner, my life was going well. I had accepted my sexual orientation, I had made a career for myself, I had a great group of friends, and I was financially stable. Marriage, I assumed, was not in the cards for me, so I grappled with the idea of having kids on my own.

I looked into adoption and in vitro fertilization (IVF), and I was open to both. A lady I spoke with at an adoption agency walked me through the timeline, and then gave me the discouraging news that it would be hard for a single person, let alone a single and LGBTQ+ person, to adopt. This was several years before same-sex marriage was legal. So I took the most realistic path forward. I was going to have a child the old-fashioned way, or actually the modern way—by using science and technology.

The IVF process could take anywhere from a few months to multiple years. I would need to undergo baseline blood tests and ultra-sounds, followed by birth control, and shots to increase the number of eggs I produced. Then, there would be a separate procedure to remove the eggs. After that, the eggs would be fertilized. If all went well, the cells would then divide to create embryos. This was followed by more shots, and another quick procedure to insert the embryo into the uterus. This sounded doable, except for the part that the egg cell needed a sperm cell.

Fortunately, there was Jack, a friend I had met during my freshman year of college.

I got to know Jack when I was eighteen. Even then, I couldn't help but think that he would be a perfect father. This was a bizarre thought to have my freshman year of college, especially because I was dating Eric at that time and I wasn't planning to have kids until I was much older. But the thought filed itself away somewhere deep in my brain. And a few months before my thirty-third birthday, I emailed Jack out of the blue to ask if he would be interested in being the father of my children. Email is my go-to for hard stuff.

When I was growing up, my mom would always say, "What is the worst that can happen?" In this case, it was Jack being unwilling to donate his sperm. So, I prepared myself for that possibility.

He called me a few days later and told me that he was honored that I had asked him. "It means a lot," he said, as his voice choked up slightly. "But I have some questions." Jack was single, too.

"Of course." The fact that he was even open to this conversation made me feel like I had won the lottery. "I'm happy to answer any questions you may have, and I really appreciate that you are even considering it," I told him.

After a week or so, Jack called me back with a list of thoughtful questions regarding the love, the well-being, and the happiness of a child that would come from him, even if he wasn't going to be raising the child.

"What are your views on raising children in a religious environment?" he asked.

"I consider myself spiritual. I will support my child if they decide to pursue religion."

He proceeded to the next question, which gave me a burst of hope that I had answered his previous question acceptably. "What type of food would you feed the child?" Jack had always been fit, and he often carried around a bottle of filtered water. It was clear he was health conscious.

"Mostly healthy, whole foods, not fast food. I definitely won't be driving through McDonald's."

He continued, "What are your views on education?"

"I've personally experienced how important education is. I would be engaged in their education, and I would make sure to provide opportunities for their learning."

He asked several more questions, anything from outdoor time to environmental consciousness. Each question confirming his remarkable character.

He finished the series of questions by letting me know that he'd love to meet any children that came out of this, and added, "When the time is right for the child, of course."

A few months later, I had several vials of his sperm stored for future use. Almost ten years later, those vials were still in storage.

25

On my first appointment at the fertility clinic, Dr. Rashid, my doctor, brought me into her office to explain the IVF process. She was all business as she pointed to a chart of the reproductive system to make things clear. It was a perfect diagram for a high school sex education class.

The statistics lesson came next with a line chart. "Your probability of getting pregnant at forty is fifty percent. At forty-two, your odds are only fifteen percent. We don't have the benefit of time on our side."

What surprised me after hearing this was that everything in my being was still, steady, and clear. I wanted to be a mother. "I understand," I said to Dr. Rashid. "What are the next steps?" Although I knew I had more work on myself to do before I could become whole, I felt a sense of peace about moving forward.

As Martin Luther King Jr. said, "Faith is taking the first step even when you don't see the whole staircase."

I trusted that, if I kept plugging away, everything would work out for the best.

A couple of months later, a heavy package arrived in a medium brown box to my house. I had recently moved back into my house from the Airbnb so there were many packages arriving lately with all the household items I had purchased. But this box was special. There were three types of medication; a bag of syringes, needles, and caps; a slew of instructions; and a red sharps container. I would need to take seven thousand dollars' worth of fertility shots every day for the next couple of weeks, in addition to a pile of medications.

I decided to start my first dose when I was in San Diego for a work trip. My brother and his wife, who was a nurse, lived there.

Asking for help, from anyone, was hard, even from a person as terrific as my brother's wife. But the fertility process was too important to let my issues or ego get in the way. My eggs were counting on me.

I texted her and asked her if she could help me.

"Absolutely," she replied.

I respected her. Besides making a difference as a nurse, she was a rock to our family. My brother rode motorcycles fast and played hard before he met her. He mellowed out after her, and they had been going strong for almost twenty years. When I saw him, which was typically once a year, he always seemed happy and affectionate. He was a responsible man, and we got along well despite there being a longstanding distance between us.

I boarded the plane to San Diego carrying a cooler packed with my fertility medication. My head was in the baby clouds the entire flight.

I met my brother and my sister-in-law at her parents' house. The kitchen table began to look like a small pharmacy as she prepped the vials and the syringes. My brother watched over her shoulder, as he showed his support. "I'm proud of you for doing this," he said.

She handed me the first syringe. "Stick the needle about an inch below and to the right of your belly button."

I took a deep breath. When I went to stick myself, my hand froze.

"I can't." The long needle looked like it would hurt.

I commanded my hand to do it, to give me the shot, but it would not budge. I tried again, and again, but my brain wasn't overriding my hand's resistance. *Who was in control here?* I couldn't blame my hand; my brain had been going rogue for months.

But eventually, my brain won, and I was able to give myself the shot. It wasn't bad, barely a pinch.

If this teensy pinch had bothered me, how would I handle a pregnancy? I pushed that thought aside. The eggs still needed to be retrieved, fertilized, tested, and stored. I had a long way to go.

26

Have I bitten off more than I can chew? So many things had begun to collide together rather than happen sequentially like I was accustomed to. Elizabeth. Claire. My divorce. My trauma. The company I worked for being acquired. My promotion. My fertility. I hadn't been able to adjust to one life change before the next one came along.

"It is the perfect storm," Janis said, unreassuringly.

"Is it a bad idea to be with Claire?"

"Do you love her?"

In truth, I wasn't in a place to love or be loved. Still, I loved her as much as I had capacity to love at the time.

"It isn't that simple. Can it work?"

Janis stared at me and her eyes seemed to say that there is nothing more important than love. "It depends how hard you two are willing to work at it, while tolerating the messiness." She kept her response practical for me.

Messes were the last thing I could tolerate.

"What can I do on my end to make it better?" I asked.

"Start by valuing your authentic self."

This sounded like pie in the sky. "Please explain."

"For starters, you need to boost yourself up rather than tear yourself down. How you treat yourself and how you treat Claire are tied together."

I nodded.

"Next, you can't let what people think dictate your life choices."

I had a lot of guilt and sadness about leaving Elizabeth and our marriage. I worried about being judged for getting a divorce and for being with someone else.

"What else do I need to work on?"

"Communication techniques," she added.

Got it. I needed to commit to do the work that a relationship takes, I had to be authentic and value myself and let go of what other people thought, and I needed to learn how to communicate.

I had enough going on; was she kidding? If I combined all of that with Claire's communication challenges, we'd have a better chance of swimming to Mars.

During one of our debacles, Claire announced that if we went ninety days without any conflict, she would tell her family about me.

This was ridiculous. It would be impossible for me to not sabotage things for ninety days. But I did my best. I didn't want to blow it. This boundary was something I defiantly wanted to try to knock down. "How about thirty days?"

"No," she responded firmly.

"Okay, forty-five days then."

I was bruised, stubborn, and determined. I tried to go under, over, around, and through those walls. Claire hardened her resolve.

"It's over. Forever," I said to her, as I hit my lowest point. The pain was written all over her face, and her chin quivered.

We had a benign friction that was sprinkled in with the big things. "You don't compost!" Claire fired at me one day, her gentle eyes flinging darts at me. She appeared more put off by my lack of composting than my toxic push-and-pull behaviors.

It *was* a contradiction, since I care about the environment. I was up on my soapbox about it, and Seattle offered a compost pickup with our regular garbage collection "What if it stinks? I don't know how," I told her.

"Take the compost out to the garbage bin before it begins to smell." She had given me a demo by opening up the small lid on her counter-top compost bin. "You put the compostable items in here, and you take the compost outside and put it in the green compost bin that's next to the trash can. Then you wheel it down to the street on trash day along with the garbage and the recycle bins."

Composting turned out to be easier than recycling, but I called her with questions. "Can you compost a banana peel?"

"Yes."

I called back two minutes later. "What about coffee grounds?"

"Yes, those too."

I called again. "And the coffee filter?"

"It's organic matter." She sounded a little perturbed.

What does organic matter even mean? I decided not to bother her again, and instead read more about it on the internet.

Despite our points of friction, she persisted by saying that she wanted us to get to the point where we could move in together and get married.

I was skeptical. How could I trust that she meant it? If she was being sincere, wouldn't she have brought me home to meet her family already? Or at least told them about me?

More importantly, how would this affect a child?

I pictured us living in her house: I would start a senseless argument with her, which would then lead to her throwing me, and my child, out into the street along with her compost bin. I would be back in an Airbnb. Maybe it would make more sense for me to buy a house in her neighborhood? This could be the right balance of proximity and distance.

Had I learned how to communicate better, I could have said, "I am committed but am struggling with so much in my life right now, and I need extra support to get through this. Can you help me navigate our relationship?" But at this time point in my journey, I'd have preferred to have been shot out of a cannon than to be that vulnerable.

Plus, the work a relationship takes was daunting when I was already therapied out. It was amazing that I had stuck to working with Janis, week after week, even as she rubbed my psyche and my emotions through a grater like a block of cheese.

My vision, the one I'd had on our first walk together, of being with Claire was beginning to unravel.

27

The sun poked through the clouds in small and big ways. My mother, my brother, his wife, and my closest friends had been there when I needed them. I continued to be touched by little everyday moments, like the heart that was drizzled in the foam of my hot chocolate that the barista at work had made me.

Yeah, my emotions were still rowdy teenagers that I was learning how to manage, but at least I could feel them now.

I decided to move forward with my IVF procedure and get my eggs retrieved. I was grateful that I had Jack's sperm and that I had the financial means to be able to do this. An anxious-looking woman in a blue sweater and her quiet partner sat in the waiting room, giving the place a somber tone.

A dry receptionist checked me in and put a bracelet on my wrist. She asked me if I had someone to drive me home, because of the anesthesia. I pointed to Claire, who stood a few feet behind me. She had adjusted her schedule to be there, but I wasn't sure if she wanted to. Either way, I was glad she was there, quietly supporting me. A nurse in teal scrubs provided me with a blue medical gown, a hairnet, and a pair of socks. I was then wheeled down the hall. The tile on the floor gleamed.

I was whisked away to a surgical room with a giant light overhead and a crew of medical staff. A mask was placed over my nose and mouth, and I was out. When I woke up, I felt disoriented. I had no idea how much time had lapsed.

Within a few moments, a nurse walked in.

"How did it go?" I asked.

"We got fourteen eggs."

That was amazing news. A smile spread on my face from ear to ear.

The nurse walked me back to the waiting room, my legs shaky, and Claire retrieved me. She dropped me off at my house, where I slept on and off the rest of the day. But I was up for most of the night, nervous and excited. I wondered how my eggs were doing, if the fertilization had worked.

The next afternoon, I leaped when I heard my phone ringing. It was the nurse.

"Ten of the eggs were fertilized," she said. "We'll call you in a few days to let you know how many of them make it."

The days felt like weeks. But finally, two days later, she called.

"Nine out of the ten made it."

Nine of my eggs are embryos! I rubbed my belly in appreciation. It felt like I had nine babies. I wasn't sure what to do about the extra embryos. It taxed my soul and my ethical framework. I was immediately attached to them, and I couldn't imagine destroying any of them. There were options for fertility patients with extra embryos. You could adopt them out or donate them to science. Although I am a fan of adoption and science, I didn't feel comfortable with either of these options. I felt a connection with all of these potential babies.

The nurse had told me that they would be sending a single cell from each embryo off for genetic testing the following day. This way, they would be able to know how many of the embryos were viable.

After another agonizing, long week, the nurse called. I held my breath. "Three of the embryos are viable," she told me.

My body surged with excitement, and tears streamed down my cheeks. *I have three babies!* This was a number I could handle.

My three babies, well, my embryos, sat on ice. They were ready as soon as I was ready. *Was I ready?* My heart was. But was my life? Bringing a child into the world was a decision that I took seriously.

Being able to provide a healthy and happy environment for a child to grow in was mandatory. I knew firsthand that if a parent wasn't ready to have a baby, this could affect the child in a negative way. Trauma is often intergenerational, frequently passed from the parent to the child. I was already going to be a single mom; could I meet the child's needs solo? How would this work with Claire? Our relationship was still new, and I had no idea where it was going.

My doctor gave me the option to move straight to the embryo transfer, but I decided not to take this route. Maybe I would be ready in another month or two, when my personal life was settled. In the meantime, my embryos would remain safely stored for future use.

28

My forty-first birthday was a few months away, and my doctor's voice periodically rang in my head. "You don't have time on your side."

"Janis, do you think I'm ready? I don't want to screw up—no offense, but I don't want my children to be in therapy for trauma when they are adults. Seriously, do you think I'll be able to provide a good home?"

"Yes." This is only one of a few times that Janis gave her direct opinion about my life choices, and I was grateful for it. Perhaps she knew my mind was already made up anyway. "Do you think you are ready?" she asked.

My gut and heart were still clear in knowing that having a child was the right path for me, but my head wanted to double-check. For one, I continued to be overwhelmed by all the emotions that I used to lock up. Also, I didn't feel secure in my relationship with Claire.

I gave myself time to do some extra soul-searching and planning. I needed to look into household help and figure out how much it would cost to take care of a child on my own if I decided not to work while the child was young. Thankfully, all the numbers added up, if I remained financially disciplined.

A month later, I sent my doctor a message. "I would like to proceed with the embryo transfer next month."

The doctor's office responded and attached a calendar with a handful of next steps. I knew the drill. Birth control, appointments, medications, and a simple procedure.

The funny thing was, I was no longer afraid. Making the decision itself was scary, but once I made it, I was excited. It didn't matter what other people thought about me or how they might judge me. I didn't care. This change was epic. Letting go of what other people thought about me allowed me to live the life that was right for me. Perhaps I should have known this because I was part of the LGBTQ+ community, but my sexual orientation wasn't a choice for me, and having a baby was.

Another month or so later, I was back in the doctor's office to have the embryo transfer. It was a simple procedure that took about ten minutes. A pedicure took longer than this. After the embryo was transferred, I immediately analyzed every sensation, pain, and tingle in my body. I scoured the internet regularly for early signs of pregnancy. It would be two weeks before I could return to the doctor's office for a pregnancy test. These were the longest two weeks of my life.

How would I take the pregnancy test result? What if it didn't work? I couldn't be alone if that happened. It would be too devastating.

I called Jody, one of my best friends from LA, and a close friend of twenty years. "Don't worry, Sara, I am flying up to be with you for this."

She provided me great comfort and distraction as we explored the city during her visit.

The night before my pregnancy test, we were hanging out in the trendy and edgy Capitol Hill neighborhood, which was alive with stores, bars, restaurants, and eclectic people buzzing about. We feasted at an amazing Asian fusion restaurant. The food smelled wonderful and looked like art on my plate, but midway through the meal, my stomach curdled. "Sorry, I have to use the restroom," I told Jody. I raced to the bathroom, and I made it just in time to expel my dinner into the toilet. My heart jumped. *This was a sign I was pregnant! Right?*

The next morning, I had my blood drawn for the pregnancy test. The day went by in slow motion as I waited the six hours for the results. I held onto my phone, and I tried not to look at it every other minute. Jody patted me on the back and gave me reassuring glances. To get my mind off things, she grabbed the purple stuffed dinosaur she had gifted Zac, and we played fetch with him on my driveway.

Around two o'clock, my phone rang. It was the doctor's office. My heart stopped and then sped back up. Cars whizzed by my driveway as I pressed my phone close to my ear. I heard the woman's voice hesitate as she introduced herself. I didn't need her to say anything. I knew the results before she said *sorry*.

Stunned, I glanced at Jody and shook my head no. In a daze, I texted Claire and told her the news. She was on vacation with her family, and I was clouding it with bad news. Or maybe the news came as a relief to her.

I ambled into the house, past Jody, who was watching me like a hawk. I sucked up the news as much as I could. *I'm not going to fall apart. I'm going to take a shower.*

But once I got in the shower, I allowed myself to sob. I cursed Janis for not being able to shut off this pain, but letting myself grieve was cathartic. I had no idea that an embryo not working would hit me so hard.

29

The doctor's office said I could wait a month before trying again, or I could try again immediately. I wanted to keep moving forward in this one area of my life—that was crystal clear.

Lucky for me, I was born with the persistence gene. When I got knocked down, I got up again, punching.

About a month later, I received another embryo transfer.

It weighed on me that I had misread my body signals during the last embryo transfer and had believed I was pregnant. In retrospect, it was possible that stress had been the cause of the vomiting. If it worked this time, if a life grew inside me, I wanted to be in touch with my body. A meaningful part of my trauma recovery was that I was now more attuned to my body.

This wasn't the first time I was out of touch with my body. I had nerve damage in my face because of ignoring major pain signals and symptoms shouting something was wrong.

A few years earlier, I was participating in endurance sports.

Keisha, a colleague in LA, suggested that I participate in a marathon with her for The Leukemia and Lymphoma Society to raise money for charity. "It will be fun," she said. I believed in the charity, and I had gained some confidence after completing my first half marathon a few months prior.

"Sure," I said. Keisha and I met for our first training session; her long, dark, muscular legs were much faster than my short, pale legs. At the end of the run, she greeted me with a bottle of cold water and peanut butter pretzels. Her bottle was already empty because she had been waiting on me for so long.

I loved the challenge and the experience. I would lace up my running shoes five days a week, and then I would jog down the hill from my house to the beach. I'd spend a moment admiring the ocean waves as they rolled up on the sparkling sand, and then, I'd take off. It was okay that even a mall walker could lap me.

Sometimes I listened to music through my earphones, while other times I would run with only the thoughts in my head. Each week, my mileage and my endurance would increase. And the thoughts in my head would slow down until, at times, they stopped. During these times, I would look at the mountains, the birds, and the coastline while I ran.

As the runs got longer—ten miles, fifteen miles, twenty miles—I had to battle thoughts that told me I was too tired to keep going. I started incorporating a mantra when I wanted to do this: *I am a runner. I am a runner.*

I wasn't. In fact, I had never been a runner. Before training for this marathon, I would only do thirty minutes on the treadmill, some weights, or a fitness class at the gym. I was now using my long-distance running as a metaphor for life, to go deeper into myself. Running also helped burn off any anxiety.

After the marathon, Keisha came into the office with a bright smile on her face and asked me if I wanted to join the Malibu triathlon team.

I said, "Okay," reasoning that the money would go to charity, too.

There were dozens of us on the team. We would have swim practice, bike rides, and group runs according to a training plan. I opted to do most of my runs and bike rides solo, but I joined the swim practices, which were coached.

The first time I got in the water, the coach told us to swim the length of the pool. I made it about five feet before he stopped me. I had never learned proper swimming techniques.

"We are going to start from the beginning," he said to me. I looked like a wet Q-tip when I looked up at him with my white plastic swim cap on. The coach had to start me as he would a toddler: "Blow bubbles."

Every week I got a little better at swimming, and my distance reached a quarter of a mile. The feeling of gliding through the water was nirvana.

It was fun, and it was amazing what my body could do. But this is when I started to ignore the signals my body was trying to communicate with me. One morning in Malibu, while I was swimming in the ocean, I heard a loud pop come from inside my neck, and I felt a sharp stab on the left side of my neck. Of course, I kept swimming and ignored it. Not only was I not listening to my body, but I was abusing it.

Leading up to the triathlon, I started to rely on my right arm and legs to pull me through the water since my left side was injured. I completed the triathlon with a nagging concern that something was wrong. I developed a burning sensation that radiated from my neck to my shoulder as my head hit the pillow at night. But I disregarded this, too. Then one morning, I woke up to find the right side of my face droopy. I tried to eat my cereal, but some of it fell out of the right side of my mouth. I went to take a drink of water, and it dripped out of my mouth. I told myself it would go away.

Weeks later, I still wasn't feeling better. I was chewing on aspirin, and I was still ignoring the red flags. *It will heal on its own*, I told myself. Now, after running a marathon, I had trouble walking a mile and it was only getting worse.

I went to the hospital, and I got an MRI. Everything was okay. My droopy face turned into facial muscle spasms. I saw a neurologist, but he couldn't pinpoint the problem and sent me to go get X-rays. I had two screwed-up disks in my neck. Now I needed to make a trip to see a surgeon. He squinted at my scans and scheduled me for surgery.

Did I take it seriously then? No. Six days after the surgery, I got on a flight to Mexico City, assuming that the recovery would be no problem. That was stupid. My body hadn't healed enough yet.

Another few weeks went by, and my neck had improved. I could walk farther and farther every day now. I even went on a hike. But the right side of my face still had muscle spasms.

It will all go away, I reassured myself. I continued on with my life. A couple years went by, and it still hadn't.

The lightbulb finally went off that I needed to take care of my body. I went to see a doctor who was an expert in facial reconstruction, including repairing nerve damage. "How long has your eye had the involuntary muscle contractions?"

"A couple years," I said, as I looked away. *Who ignores such an obvious physical problem for so long?*

"That's a long time. It will get better, but it will be a slow process. It could take years, but make sure you stick with it."

Every few months, the doctor would insert shots of Botox under my right eye to keep the damaged nerve area from firing out of control and to slowly alter and rewire the nerve function in my face. As a bonus, this area of my face, which was about the size of a quarter, had no fine lines or wrinkles. Though I was tempted to get injections all over my face, I stayed with the medical plan and vowed to be on top of my health moving forward.

The message was clear: listen to your body and take care of it as soon as it signals that something is off.

Although it was absurd how long I had ignored my body, it could have been worse. I'm fortunate to be able to live an active lifestyle again. But I'm more compassionate toward my body, slowing down or stopping if something feels off and not pushing it toward mileage goals.

After my first embryo transfer failed, I took some time to observe and scan my body. It felt ready. I remained grounded in my decision. But this time, I wanted to find a gentler approach for my body to the embryo transfer. I chose a natural transfer, which meant no shots.

The second procedure was about ten minutes and went as unceremoniously as the first one. After the procedure, I relaxed into the two-week wait for the pregnancy test.

30

Over the next two weeks, I welcomed how busy things were at work, which included a trip to New York. While I was there, I visited a friend of mine who was about six months pregnant and was having her own relationship issues. It was stressful to hear about the conflicts that she and her partner were having, and I confessed to her the challenges I was having with Claire. We were able to support each other, which brought both of our stress levels down a notch.

On the flight back home, I felt a few funny sensations in my stomach, but I didn't vomit. I also didn't get my hopes up, and instead, I shifted my focus to work.

The days until I was back in the doctor's office for another pregnancy test inched closer. I kept myself so busy while waiting for the call with the results that I missed the call from the doctor's office. Luckily, they left me a voice mail message. My heart was racing as I waited to hear it play.

"Hi, this is Cindy from Seattle Reproductive Medicine." Her voice sounded positive, or at least, not regretful. And then the magic words. "Your pregnancy test came back positive."

The world stopped, and I broke down in tears of joy. I paced, digesting the news, and more tears fell. It felt like I had climbed Mount Everest, and now, I could finally enjoy the spectacular view.

I texted Claire. "It worked!" Reaching out to her felt weird; I had no idea what role she would—or wanted to—play in my pregnancy or with the baby. Things continued to be bumpy with us.

She called and congratulated me and later gave me a card and gift.

I reached out to my mom, who had to muzzle herself not to shout the news from the rooftops, but I told her to wait until the second trimester. She only slipped a few times, which was impressive for her.

I started reading books about pregnancy, I researched daycares, and I started a list of baby names. And I continued to clean and reorganize my house.

It was time for me to tell my unborn baby's father that it had worked. I emailed Jack, and he called me with enthusiasm and support from both himself and his wife. He had gotten married a few years after he donated the most generous gift I had ever received. "My wife and I are happy for you, and if something were to ever to happen to you, we are fully willing to take on the parental responsibilities and raise the child. No pressure, just an offer. Whatever you feel is best." This meant so much to me. The more people to love the baby, the better.

31

Weeks after I learned I was pregnant, I went to Claire's house for her birthday dinner. This was my first time seeing her in a week, and I was determined to be a good birthday date and make a positive impression on her friends. Although I had met them before, they knew I had been crappy to Claire, and I worried they wished she had never met me. They were kind people, and it was fair for them to be protective of their friend.

I looked through my closet in search of a nice outfit, but my olive-green pants were too tight, and my blue too loose; the black pants were too dressy, and the white ones too casual; the black shirt was too trendy, and the white button-up shirt not trendy enough. Zac lay on the floor, watching me with curiosity. Finally, I settled on black heels, jeans, and a black silk shirt with an Asian collar.

I got into my car and gave myself a pep talk like it was halftime and my team was down by three touchdowns. But as soon as I started driving, my lunch rose to my throat and I had to pull off the road to throw up. Morning sickness. I texted Claire from a gas station parking lot where I stopped to buy breath mints and Pepto to tell her that I would be there in a few minutes. As bad luck would have it, there was a car fire, and her exit was shut down. I was stressed as I detoured to the next exit.

Claire hugged me when I arrived, almost thirty minutes late, and I noticed that her friends were in clusters around the living room. One seemed to scowl at me. Was I imagining this? *Quit being self-conscious,* I willed myself.

Pasting a nervous smile on my face, I trembled over to a cluster of four ladies. They were telling stories of the old days. I listened for a few minutes, but having little to add, I made my way over to another cluster. There were two men and a woman, and I racked my brain for an icebreaker. The best I could come up with was, "So, how did you get into your line of work?" This was awkward. A stereotypical question.

Everyone had a glass of wine, but because I was pregnant, I couldn't have the relief of alcohol. I drank a glass of water, and no one asked me why I wasn't drinking wine, which was a relief, since it was still too early to announce that I was pregnant.

The dinner was a lovely four-course meal of lobster-tart appetizers, puréed butternut squash soup, salt-crusted tilapia, and dark chocolate ganache accompanied by wine pairings. A chef had prepared it in Claire's kitchen.

The dinner table conversation made its way to the trials and tribulations of online dating. Apparently, some men thought it okay to send a picture of their genitals.

My insides tightened. As a woman who was too reserved to talk about sexuality publicly, I had no idea how to wiggle my way into the conversation.

Claire left the room for a while, and I felt panicked. Her friend who scowled when I first arrived finally looked at me. She continued to lead a conversation about a girls trip they all had planned for the following weekend. I had nothing to contribute to that conversation, either. All I could think about was being back in the safety and comfort of my bed, wrapped in blankets.

One couple left the party after dessert, which paved the way for me to leave soon, too. One of Claire's family members, who didn't know we were dating, was staying in one of the guest bedrooms, so I didn't need to worry about being asked to spend the night. I left the party as early as I could without appearing rude.

Back at home, safely under my covers, I told myself it was over. I didn't feel safe with her. As wrong as my sabotaging behaviors were, I did them all to find some reassurance that I could trust her.

In order to have the healthiest and most peaceful body for my baby to develop in, I needed to reduce the stress in my life, and this relationship was stressful. Not just for me, but for Claire, too.

I picked up the phone and called my mom.

"Mom, it didn't work out with Claire. Can you come here?"

"Keep your chin up," she said, and she flew out to Seattle the next day.

She was here for me.

In truth, letting go wasn't quick or easy. Once I gathered enough belief in myself and courage to be vulnerable, I came crawling back. I decided to give it everything I had. I harassed her with too many flowers, apology emails, and promises to count. I was trying too hard to prove to her and to myself that I was worth another chance, and I fought my heart out by keeping it exposed, even though it meant coming face-to-face with my fears—rejection and abandonment.

Go figure, my fears came true. Claire rejected me and ran over my naked heart with a semi-truck. However, in fairness to her, my fireball approach had burned through her boundaries.

We met in person for a conversation, and it was a positive one. I did my best to apologize for the things I had done wrong, empathize, and acknowledge my mistakes. I wished her well. I meant this. It's not to say that the rejection didn't suck. It really sucked. Or that I didn't feel anger, heartache, or grief—I experienced these excruciating feelings intensely. But I'm grateful I am able to feel and sit with my emotions, even the hard ones.

Claire told me that she had tried hard, which she had, and that my trauma was too much for her and she didn't have the capacity. This wasn't surprising because that is what I sensed from the beginning. I acknowledged how difficult it must have been for her, and that I, too, hadn't had the capacity to support her because I was so absorbed with healing, divorce, and fertility.

I was also honest with her. I told her that I did the best I could. My healing process entailed going in circles as I worked to break my negative behaviors and patterns. No matter how much I wanted to fix my issues, I could not resolve them as fast as I wanted to. When someone is working through complex post-traumatic stress disorder, both people in the relationship need to make an informed decision about whether to be in the relationship.

Being triggered is no excuse to treat anyone poorly, and it was on me to figure out how to be consistently emotionally available in a relationship. At the same time, if she was more trauma informed, there were a few things she could have done differently that would have alleviated my stress and helped my triggers to be more manageable. At the end of the day, Claire had the right to look out for her needs.

She offered me friendship, which I seriously considered, but in the end, the friendship I wanted to focus on was the one with myself.

All was far from lost. The shocking thing about diving headfirst into one of your greatest fears is that you learn what happens when that fear comes true. I did get rejected by Claire, and in the end, I was okay. I didn't reject myself, which is what mattered most. The other success from our failed relationship was that I got practical lessons to take with me into my future relationships, such as learning how to communicate better and how to respect boundaries.

32

My mom arrived in Seattle more excited than I had ever seen her. When I picked her up at the airport, she bounced up to my car and her hand went straight for my stomach. "Hi, grandbaby!" she shrieked hello to my little bean. Having her there lifted my spirits after my breakup with Claire. She would end up staying with me for more than half of my pregnancy and providing support.

Janis also provided wisdom about my breakup through her questions and challenges. "Why do you blame yourself for things not working out with Claire? She contributed to the problems in the relationship, too." It was rare to see mild-mannered Janis flare up. Did I hit a hot button? Janis told me a problem she has to look out for is that people who have had trauma can shoulder too much of the blame in many areas of their lives. I 100 percent agree with Janis that a victim is never to blame for trauma. The thing is, Claire didn't abuse me. She wasn't trauma informed enough to support me and was reasonably doing what she needed to do.

I fired back at Janis. "I don't blame myself for everything! How is it useful to sit here and tell you about the things I think she did wrong? It does not feel empowering for me to do that. It is empowering to focus on what I could have done differently so I can work on doing stuff better in the future." Of course, I was upset that Claire didn't think the juice was worth the effort of the squeeze. But I chose to focus on what I can do better moving forward.

Janis nodded and began giving me pointers on communication skills and boundaries.

After I got home, crabby from my session with Janis, my mom was pulling a batch of chocolate chip cookies out of the oven that she baked for her grandbaby. "Mom, I have to eat healthy during my pregnancy," I whined. But I took a warm, gooey cookie and was glad she was there.

There was a lot of work to be done preparing for my new arrival. I hobbled into my office one wonderfully ordinary day, and my boss offered to expand my role. I told her, "No thanks." Passing up the opportunity to expand my responsibilities was monumental for me. I had never said no at work—proof that I was a recovering workaholic. My priorities had become clear to me. Maintain a healthy womb for my baby to develop in, take care of my dog, and spend time with my mom—my family.

The only thing I allowed to expand was my waistline. And wow, did it expand. At the beginning of my pregnancy, I jogged and walked around five miles a day. As the pregnancy progressed, my running turned to walking, and my walking turned to waddling. I ended up gaining forty-seven pounds, which was a huge amount for me as I had averaged 125 pounds since high school. But all that mattered was that my baby was growing well.

My mom was staying in my guest room, and we were getting along well. But I still had pent-up anger and resentment that would seep through, and I would get annoyed with her even over positive things. I went as far as blaming her.

If she hadn't been so messed up when she was raising me, I wouldn't be having a baby alone and single, as she had. I was incapable of making a relationship work because of her.

I stored my anger away. I could deal with it in the future; I didn't want bad vibes around my growing baby. So I focused on the good things about my mother. *She has a huge heart, she is so excited about the baby, she is funny.* And although I had put my anger away, I didn't push it away. I noticed the subtle difference of this. Rather than freezing emotions out, I was connecting to them and managing them.

Janis had told me that no emotions are bad. Even anger is good. All emotions have a purpose. And you can get to a point beyond managing them and begin to harness them.

She sounded like Yoda, but this didn't quite make sense. I asked her to explain to me how anger was a good emotion.

"For one, it is a powerful force that can motivate and mobilize a person. It can be a warning system that something is off, like a response to one of your boundaries being violated. And it can give a person deep self-insight if they peel back the layers to discover what deeper emotions are happening under the anger."

My mom also continued to provide me comfort during this time. "I just want you to be happy," was all she'd say about my failed marriage and relationship. And I knew she meant it.

I hoped to support my own child in this way, to unconditionally love and accept whatever path in life they chose.

"Mom, we have to go!" I yelled, as I ran down the stairs in my stretchy yoga pants.

"I'm ready." She was already waiting at the front door, early and responsible. She was wearing the nice outfit she had packed: purple dress pants, a white sweater with sequins, and leather loafers.

It was ultrasound day. The technician squinted at me while my mom and I held our breath. "Your baby is measuring in the ninety-fifth percentile." How was I going to squeeze the baby out when I went into labor? My obstetrician was already cautious because I was a geriatric patient at forty-one. All my cravings for gallons of milk and plates of spaghetti had paid off.

"Your baby looks very healthy," the doctor said to me when she read the ultrasound. And in the end, that is what mattered, not the weight I had put on or the fact that my ankles had swelled up like water balloons. *My baby was healthy!* I let out a sigh of relief. I had done all right so far. And as long as I kept it up for the next eighteen years, my child would be okay.

33

Zac was zipping around the park with a stick in his mouth. He had no idea his life was about to change. A lady standing near me had a baby strapped around her chest in a carrier while her dog also played in the park. It was exciting to think that this would be me in a few months.

"How old is your baby?" I asked her. Generally, I was introverted but becoming a parent, in addition to the work I had done with Janis, made me a little more outgoing.

"She's four months." The woman smiled. "When are you due?"

"In May," I told her.

We chatted away about the first few months of motherhood and pregnancy. "I did prenatal yoga classes at Aditi a couple of times a week," she told me. "It's a wonderful community of women."

I had no experience with yoga, but it seemed like a good thing to do now that most other forms of exercise were off the table. I also knew that yoga connected people to what was happening in their body, which is one of many PTSD treatment approaches. Yoga is a common intervention in recovery, as trauma is often stored and stuck in the body and can manifest through physical problems.

I walked into a lobby area that was filled with plants and nature sounds coming from speakers in the ceiling. A middle-aged woman with a sun tattoo, a beaded necklace, and incredibly straight posture, greeted me warmly. "Welcome to Aditi. I haven't seen you before. Do you need a tour?"

She walked me into the large community room where yogis set up their mats and then guided me to the bathroom. "It's very important to know where this is, especially for our pregnant yogis," she added. After the tour, she handed me a schedule of the prenatal classes.

I went a couple times each week. About twenty women sat on cushions around the room, their hands usually resting on their basketball-sized bellies. Each session started with us introducing ourselves by name, due date, and something that was currently on our mind.

Our group bonded in no time, especially as we got to know and encourage each other. This was the first new community I had become part of since retreating into my shell after my marriage fell apart. I really appreciated how these women embraced new people and allowed each other to be vulnerable.

They bravely shared the good, the bad, and the ugly, their hopes and their fears. Everyone noticed when a woman was no longer in class. How thrilled we all were when our instructor said, "Shonda just had her baby. It was a girl." We were all happy for the new mothers that graduated, and we were hopeful that we would see them, and meet their babies, when we advanced to postnatal yoga.

After we did our sharing, we did some simple stretches: cat and cow to wake up our spine and ease our back pain, legs-up-the-wall to help with swollen ankles, side stretches to encourage more space in our crowded abdomen. My baby, presumably participating in class, too, kicked my ribs periodically to add some extra pizzazz.

Deep breathing and mindfulness were an important part of the practice. "In and out, slowly and deeply, through the nose," the teacher guided us. "To a count of four." She had us focus on becoming aware of the sensations in our bodies.

She said, "As you become more aware of your body's sensations, you feel yourself becoming more attuned with your mind and body." *This was exactly what I needed!* Trauma creates disconnection from the body. Yoga creates self-awareness and connection. This connection extended beyond the body. It expanded to an interconnected community beyond the mat.

One day, Lily, who was ready to pop, asked me to join her and a few others after class for lunch.

I told her that I would love to, hoping she didn't go into labor at lunch.

We headed over to a bistro down the street. While one woman chomped on a cheeseburger and another on a salad, Lily and I had a plate of pasta each. We discussed what everyone was doing for exercise in addition to yoga. The answers were walking and napping.

We then started discussing what everyone was buying to prepare for their new arrivals.

"This is a safe infant car seat." Lily showed me a picture of a gray car seat on her phone. "And the fire department will check to make sure that our car seats are installed properly." This was new information for me, and I added a car seat safety check to my to-do list.

The social support made a big difference in helping us understand the changes that were happening in our bodies and in our lives as we prepared to transition into motherhood.

Why hadn't I joined a support group in my healing journey? This was an opportunity.

34

The thought of moving on with my life as if my marriage had never happened bothered me. The regret for hurting Elizabeth gnawed at me, and I missed her and her family. How could I have so quickly dismissed the person with whom I shared so much love and so many memories? The person I grew with, the person with whom my life was calm and peaceful?

Many states have waiting periods before a divorce is finalized. My attorney reached out after that mandatory waiting period was over for our divorce to be finalized. My heart was as heavy as lead. Was this it? Would I ever see Elizabeth again? I assumed Elizabeth would never want to see me again, but I wanted to talk to her. I reached out to her, and she graciously agreed to meet with me.

We met at a local park within walking distance from both our houses—she had moved into a new place nearby. She arrived with Leo, while Zac sat next to me.

My eyes filled up with tears when I saw her.

We spoke for hours. I tried to explain why I shut down, and why I had walked out of our marriage so abruptly. I also filled her in on my PTSD work.

Elizabeth nodded and listened intently before she spoke. "I was in shock when you left. It still doesn't make sense." She looked confused, and my words started getting stuck in my head.

I had trouble explaining it all. "I don't feel like I am explaining the trauma part well. You are welcome to join me at an appointment with Janis if you would like more information on that?" Janis could try to help me explain to Elizabeth what had happened.

"Okay," she replied. We both reasoned that it could help us both learn and grow. Elizabeth had also been doing her own personal growth work, and it showed. She talked about her feelings—anger, hurt, betrayal—and asked questions. She shared with me that she had indeed wanted kids, and she also shared with me the things that frightened her about it. She took part of the responsibility for our failed relationship when I blamed it all on myself.

A few days later, we met in front of Janis's office. Janis, expecting both of us, was as ready as a college professor to provide Elizabeth with an overview of PTSD. She pulled out her yellow legal pad and drew a diagram of the brain. She pointed her pen at the different regions to show how PTSD affected behavior, the brain, and the nervous system. "When Sara left, she was in an acute state of PTSD. She was flooded with symptoms and disassociated from her emotions."

Elizabeth listened carefully.

"When Sara first came to see me, she said she felt like she was offline. This is an accurate analogy for the disconnection that can happen."

I chimed in. "This doesn't make what I did okay." I realized that what Janis was saying was more of an explanation than an excuse. The work I was doing with her weekly was a form of personal responsibility. While I didn't know if Elizabeth or my other exes I left would forgive me, I realized doing this work on myself was one step in the right direction toward making amends.

Elizabeth asked questions, and Janis discussed many of the concepts she had explained to me.

Overall, the appointment felt positive and constructive. We were both silent as we walked out of Janis's office and got in the elevator. It had been a heavy conversation with a lot to process. When the elevator doors opened to the lobby Elizabeth asked me if I wanted to get something to eat.

Eating had become one my favorite things to do lately, and I swear, the baby kicked excitedly at the suggestion of another meal. I rubbed my tummy to let the little kicker know we were on the same page.

We walked to a café and continued to discuss what we were both working on and what went wrong in our marriage.

A few days later, we met again for brunch at a restaurant in between both of our places to continue to talk. It was clear that we had both been on personal growth journeys and, while neither of us wished divorce on ourselves, we were able to see that the silver lining of it was to learn from it, if we chose to do so.

The next time I saw Janis, I thanked her for talking to Elizabeth, and I filled her in on brunch.

"I feel comfortable talking to her. Maybe I shouldn't have given up on our marriage," I said to Janis.

"There is a small percentage of people who regret their divorce. It's normal."

That word again. *Normal.*

"There is a field within couples counseling that's called discernment counseling. Think of it as divorce counseling. It is designed to help a couple learn from everything they went through and to help them figure out one of two paths. If they should go their separate ways, or if they should work on their relationship." Janis scribbled the name and phone number of a discernment counselor on a sheet of paper.

The thought of spending more time in counseling gave me hives. I still had an aversion to counseling and saw it as a crutch. If my leg was broken, I wouldn't have a problem using crutches, but the shame and stigma around not "just getting over it" was something I still struggled with.

35

As I neared the end of my pregnancy, my huge belly making some tasks more difficult, Elizabeth started helping me with household chores and carrying my shopping bags. As we put the groceries away, I mentioned the idea of discernment counseling. She was game.

Two weeks later, we were meeting with a counselor who went over the usual overview of how her practice worked and disclaimers. She added one caveat: "I don't do discernment counseling if there was any domestic abuse or substance abuse. If either of those things are happening, I generally think divorce is a sound decision." Elizabeth and I never had any issues with abuse of any kind during our relationship, so we were in the clear, but her comment really made me think about divorce, especially my mom's divorce from Earl. Although Earl had been hooked on drugs, he was redeemable.

However, I respected the counselor's policy, just as I respected my mom's decision to call it quits. Divorce can certainly be the right decision for different people, and for different reasons, and it's none of my business what people decide is right for them anyway.

It hit me that my thinking had become more gray and less judgmental. This was a good sign, because according to Janis, one unhealthy pattern of people with trauma is that thinking can be black-and-white.

The counselor also shared that about one in four couples regret getting divorced. And that about one in ten remarry the partner they were married to.

The counselor didn't seem like she was acting, which was another good sign. And Elizabeth and I were actually able to talk deeply about the stuff that hurt our marriage and glean insights.

When we spent time together, Elizabeth and I would play board games for entertainment, even though I couldn't push my chair up to the table because of my protruding stomach. Elizabeth would have to walk around the table when it was time to get up and pull me up by my hands, so that I didn't have to struggle to get myself up.

She would eyeball my belly and ask, "Are you thirsty? Are you hungry? Want to go for a walk?"

It was so strange. Her ambivalence about having kids was a wedge between us. And now she was seemingly as excited as I was.

We hung out mostly at her place and then at mine, the one that was formerly ours. At first, being in our old house together again felt overwhelming. But gradually, we were comfortable in it again. As my due date approached, Elizabeth started spending nights in our former home. My body was so uncomfortable that I couldn't sleep, and I was nervous that I would roll over wrong and hurt the baby.

We discussed her moving back into the house. We weren't sure where this path would lead. But it was a path forward. Now that I was okay with the gray, I was okay with not knowing. We took things day by day.

Zac was so excited to have another dog around, and he tried to wrestle with Leo. Leo, our elderly beagle, who spent most of the day sleeping in his cow-patterned dog bed, would lift his head and growl at Zac until he backed off. But within a couple of weeks, they were both curled up in the same bed.

36

I was no longer experiencing flashbacks or nightmares anymore, but waking up in a puddle of water—now, that was disturbing.

My water had broken in the middle of the night. It took me a minute to realize I was having mild cramps, unaware that these were contractions. I tried to leap out of bed, but I was stuck on my side and had to slowly pull my body up.

I yelped to Elizabeth, as I was walking around the room in circles trying to figure out what to do next. Should I shower? Should I clean up the mess from my water breaking? This was not the time to worry about cleaning anything. I needed to get to the hospital.

"Get in the car," Elizabeth instructed.

My mind went blank. I couldn't remember anything I had learned from the baby classes. I took a series of classes to prepare, including a two-day course that went over the entire labor and delivery process, and I remembered nothing.

"Should I call ahead?" I asked.

Elizabeth shrugged. "We'll call from the car."

A couple of minutes later, we were trying to get into the car but neither of us had the keys. Elizabeth ran back into the house to get them.

The drive to the hospital was taking too long. "Should I run this light?" Elizabeth asked me, as we sat at a red light. There were no cars in sight because it was two in the morning.

"Yes, hurry!" I commanded, worried the baby would pop out on the car seat.

We screeched into the ER and hurried into the hospital. The staff remained calm as they wheeled me into the labor and delivery department. After helping me get into a bed, they hooked me up to a monitor. A nurse examined me and told me I wasn't dilated yet.

"This will take a while. Your job now is to go for a walk."

I looked at Elizabeth. "I guess we didn't need to run the red light."

She laughed. "This will give me time to go back and get the suitcase." We had forgotten the packed bag at home in our rush to get out of the house.

After eight hours, I still wasn't dilated. The nurse gave me a drug to help. Twelve hours later, I still wasn't where I needed to be. I took more drugs. Twelve hours after that, still little dilation. They put a monitor on my baby, and my eyes were glued to the screen with the baby's vitals. After thirty-two hours of labor, I had grown concerned about my baby's head trying to get through the narrow birth canal. I was attuned enough to my body that I could feel that the situation was concerning.

I called the nurse in, and she told me that she would give me more drugs to dilate me.

"No," I demanded. "Call the doctor. We need to get the baby out now." And, sure enough, the baby's heart rate soon started to show signs of distress.

Minutes later, I was being prepped for a C-section.

They wheeled me into the operating room, and the medical staff swarmed around me.

I was terrified. *Is my baby going to be okay? What if I don't make it?* I closed my eyes and pleaded. "God, please protect my baby. Take me if it means my baby will be okay." I had an estate plan already drawn up, and great people who would happily raise my baby if needed, along with instructions for my family and closest friends, if anything were to ever happen.

The medical team worked quickly and expertly. I felt some tugging as they pulled the baby out, and a moment later, I heard a cry. *My baby was okay.* Elizabeth was standing over by the doctors and nurses, monitoring everything like a detective as they inspected and weighed him. I was shaking on the operating table from all the pain medication

I had been given, holding back my tears so I could see him. My heart was exploding with joy.

A few minutes later, on April 30, 2018, I was holding Maximilian, my perfect, healthy baby boy. He had the tiniest hands and feet, chubby cheeks, and the shortest, softest hair I have ever felt.

He lay contently on my chest, his hazel eyes half open, as I held him close. I stroked my hand across his forehead, down his cheeks, on his back.

Poor little guy had gone from the warm, rhythmic, and controlled world in my belly to the chaos of a hospital room—bright lights, beeping machines, nurses coming and going—but he didn't seem to mind at all. He was chill and happy to just eat, sleep, and be held.

When I was back in my room, with the shades down to darken it, Max was swaddled and asleep. The nurse offered to wheel him to the nursery overnight so I could sleep after thirty-two hours of labor.

But I told her that I was okay.

There was no way I would allow Max to be wheeled off to a strange room far away from me. I pulled the hospital bassinet up against my bed, and I rested my right hand on him as I slept for a couple of hours.

I awoke to see him in Elizabeth's arms. She was staring at him with googly eyes. She got up and handed him to me, though it was clear that she, too, didn't want to let go of him.

In the days following my release from the hospital, Max and I were showered with love. My chest swelled as I watched people hold and love him.

My family and Elizabeth's family all came to visit. They would hover over him as they waited for their turn to hold him. He ate well, he would quiet when he was held, and he fell asleep easily.

When he fussed, I carried him off to the bedroom to nurse him, and if that didn't work, I would carry him outside. He loved the outdoors. He was naturally at peace in the fresh air.

Elizabeth took care of us. She brought me meals, did our laundry, and washed the dishes.

Like a protective bear, I kept my eye on everyone who held Max. *Did they wash their hands? Were they supporting his neck correctly?*

I spotted danger everywhere. *What if that shelf falls? Was he placed correctly into the car seat? Was he breathing okay?* I slept with one eye open, and I watched him eat, sleep, poop, and grow.

This was the first time in my life that I had put another living being before myself. Sure, we all do things to put other people first. You want to see one movie, your partner wants to see a different movie, so you compromise and watch the movie they want to see.

But with my son it was different. It was all about him. He had to eat every two to three hours, and I dropped whatever I was doing when he seemed hungry. It was primal. It was radical. I quickly learned to read his cues and respond to them. I never realized how self-absorbed I was before Max came along.

I went to see Janis shortly after Max was born, and he slept in my arms. "I'm worried about everything," I told her.

She told me that this was how most new mothers felt. But I wanted to know how my background would affect me as a mother.

She explained, from her experience, the two risks that parents who had experienced trauma in their childhoods need to be on the lookout for. One risk was not protecting their children adequately and passing along the trauma to their own kids. The other risk was that some parents were too protective, hovering constantly. Janis said that she wasn't worried about me not meeting Max's needs; her hunch was that I was at risk of being the latter kind of parent, and I would need to watch out to not be overly protective of him. Luckily, I had time to figure that out because he was a newborn, and I wanted to be with him 24/7 and hover for now.

I thought about not going back to therapy after I had Max, figuring I could resolve any remaining issues on my own from here. But I realized that it was probably a good idea to have people like Janis as a sounding board as I parented Max.

At his three-month checkup, Max was smiling and cooing at the doctor and the nurse as I laid him on the table for vaccines. I braced myself, and Elizabeth teared up, as they injected the shots. Max's eyes got big, I thought he was going to cry, but then he gave the nurse a big smile. "What a happy little fella," the doctor said.

The pediatrician gave a thumbs-up and said, "He is a happy and healthy baby. And a big guy, too." Max had gained ten ounces since his last appointment and was around the ninety-fifth percentile in weight.

I exhaled a sigh of relief, and my confidence grew, too.

37

I dressed Max in a onesie that looked like overalls, while he wiggled and cooed with sparkly eyes.

After my positive experience with the yoga moms, I signed up for a moms group. I was excited to have a group of new moms to connect with and to ask questions to.

During our first meeting, I joined nine other women who were sitting on chairs and couches in a circle. They were holding blue, yellow, or pink bundles of hope and promise in their arms. The oldest baby was around two months old. I looked down at Max, who was sleeping on my stomach, and lit up when I thought about how lucky I was.

The moms had that newborn aura of joy mixed with a haggard, sleepless look. I'm sure I did as well. We still looked a few months pregnant because our stomachs hadn't shrunk down yet. At this point, I had lost about twenty-five pounds and was on my way to losing all the weight I had gained. I had attributed the weight loss to running around changing diapers and my daily walks with Max.

After the facilitator introduced us, we went around the circle doing introductions, and then, we shared our stories.

Most stories were about how happy the mothers felt—until one brave woman spoke her truth. Her baby slept no more than an hour or two at a time. He cried through the night and needed to be held all the time. In the middle of the night, she and her husband would be in their car, driving the newborn around the neighborhood.

"He still cries all the time," she said, shedding a few tears. The adorable blue bundle was in his infant seat, quiet as a church mouse, which was a relief for his mother.

Her vulnerability gave all of us, or me at least, courage. We all have our ups and downs, and this mom's honesty made me realize that I could open up. Just not at the first meeting. I would have to develop trust with this group, which wasn't my default setting.

The facilitator asked us to share our birth stories next. Some of the ladies bared their souls. The stories varied from natural childbirth to epidurals and C-sections; from short births that took a few hours to long, painful ones that seemed like they would never end. Hearing all of these private details from strangers felt weird. I was such a private person, and I knew I needed to shed some skin.

I kept it brief when it was my turn to share. "My delivery was long. Thirty-two hours of labor was then followed by an unplanned C-section. But the minute I heard Max cry, all was forgotten."

That was it. I didn't share a thing about how he was conceived or about my personal life.

I beat myself up for not being more open about Elizabeth, and how we had recently reconciled. I wondered if they assumed Elizabeth and I were a model same-sex couple: Elizabeth running around changing Max's diapers, swaddling him, and wearing him in a sling around her chest while I did housework or slept. We truly were a great team.

"I was scared and excited," said the next mom. "I had to get a C-section, even though I had planned for a natural birth." Tears welled up in her eyes as she continued to authentically share about her experience.

Understanding, empathy, and support oozed from the group. There was no judgment or unsolicited advice. I chilled out; joining this group had been the right decision.

After that first meeting, I looked forward to our weekly meetings. People shared stories about the death of loved ones, friction at home, and what it feels like to watch your baby grow. Eventually, these women would break through my protective layer.

"We moved our son out of our room into a crib in his own room," Rebecca shared, her eyes with a hint of sadness in them. "I lie awake knowing that he will move farther and farther from me as he grows."

I quickly swallowed the lump in my throat. I could relate.

Max slept in a bassinet right next to my bed, and I loved watching him sleep. When he was ready to move into his crib in his own room, I stood over the rails watching him as he settled in peacefully. I missed him when he was in a different room. I was concerned I wouldn't hear him if he needed me, even though I had a monitor right next to both of our beds. When it was time for me to go to bed, I went in his room and slept on an air mattress by his crib.

The next night, I moved him back to his bassinet next to my bed for another month before trying the crib a second time. Heartache and worry washed over me as I retreated to my own room. Again, I inflated the air mattress and slept next to his crib.

Elizabeth tried to comfort me "He is okay in his room. His crib has to be more comfortable than the bassinet." She was attached too and wore him in a wrap on her chest while she did things around the house. He'd stick out his head out like a baby kangaroo his its mother's pouch and take in all the excitement around him—that was, until his eyes got heavy.

I protested. "He is literally sleeping attached to your body." She had a good point, though. The mattress in the bassinet was thin compared to his thick crib mattress, so I ripped the Band-Aid off and he slept in his own room.

Unlike Max, who slept like a champ anywhere, I stirred all night in my sleep the first night he was in his own room. I couldn't help it. Babies were meant to be close to their mothers so they could be protected. As Max grew, the other mothers became a helpful sounding board, along with Janis, who had a lot of education in developmental psychology.

I worried about being overprotective, overcorrecting from all the freedom I'd had during my childhood. I wanted to find the right balance of providing protection and support, along with autonomy.

Max was on his playmat with a few toys, and he had gotten himself up into a tripod position. He bobbled a bit. I had an impulse to scoop him up, but I fought it off. A few seconds later, he was sitting for the first time, wobbling and swaying, until he tipped on his side. He looked at me with big eyes, and my heart panicked as I reached for him. Then he started to giggle and pushed himself back into sitting position. Falling was part of his learning, and I had to figure out the right amount of space to give him so he could learn and explore his world.

The other fear that I had been dealing with was how it would mentally or emotionally affect Max if things soured with Elizabeth. Janis had told me that the more positive people that are around and love a child, the better. Elizabeth was both positive and loved Max, but I was still nervous. Janis scribbled down another name and number on the back of one of her cards. It was the contact information for one of the best early-childhood psychologists in the region. This was psychologist number six in the two years since I'd walked out on my marriage, and I was ready to cut the cord on leveraging experts for help.

I took Max to the appointment, where he played with a rattle and a doll while the child psychologist interacted with him. He smiled at the psychologist and then at the baby doll he had been given. I went to two more appointments, without Max, and asked him a ton of questions and sought his advice. Like Max's pediatrician, the psychologist increased my confidence when he said, "Max seems healthy, happy, and securely attached. It is clear to me how much he is loved and wanted and cared for." My shoulders loosened up with this news, and I started to relax into motherhood. He continued, "It doesn't matter if you and Elizabeth end up together or not. Parents staying together or splitting up in itself, doesn't necessarily negatively affect a child's health and well-being. What matters is that a child's caregiver provides consistent love and safety. You both do that. In fact, the more people that love him the better." He echoed what Janis had said.

This soothed my nerves. Elizabeth and her entire family loved him to pieces.

He went on to give some additional advice. "Divorce, grief, and loss are a part of life. For instance, Max could lose a grandparent when he's young, and what will matter most for Max's well-being is how you show up for him when his life challenges or his transitions happen. If he is given extra support during those times, then he will be okay. In fact, if handled right, adversity could increase his levels of resilience and can ultimately be positive for him."

This validated a belief I had from my own experiences—some adversity can be good. There were some traits that I was glad I'd developed from my childhood. Not to minimize that adversity can cause trauma and have harmful consequences, but adversity itself does not have to cause trauma.

Elizabeth and I took all this information to heart. We had many conversations, though some conversations were really tough, about our unified commitment to Max if we didn't make it. We were both on the same page: Max's well-being would be our top priority. She and her family had loved him since day one. And I was confident, no matter what, they would always be there for him.

At the last parents group meeting, our babies scattered on a large baby blanket together chewing on teethers or shaking toys, I felt brave enough to be vulnerable—only vaguely, but it was a start. I shared about how Elizabeth and I had some difficulties, and that I was in counseling working some stuff out. I told them that it was hard not knowing our fate.

I continued by telling them how much I admired them, and how much I had learned from them. Things like how to give and receive support, how to transition Max from milk to solid food, how to laugh and feel joy at everyone's ups, and how to be present and compassionate in our downs.

The group was cool, and we pivoted the new moms group to a book club. We've stuck together to this day. Afterward, one of the mothers pulled me aside to get the contact information for the counselor I mentioned, which reminded me how universal our struggles are.

38

When Max was five months old, it was time to either transition back to work or quit my job.

As the days got closer, I held Max a little tighter. Having been with him constantly since the day he was born, the thought of separating from him crushed me. How would I be able to be away from him for twenty hours a week, and then forty hours a week later in the year? Should I quit my job? This, coming from a workaholic.

I decided to return to work. Max attended La Escuelita, a Spanish immersion preschool filled with warm, kind teachers. Max was in the baby room with six other babies and three teachers.

The first day I dropped him off, I stalked the building and peered into the window of his classroom. He was sitting on a playmat playing with a wooden play cube. A few minutes later, Elsa, one of the teachers, picked him up. He looked safe and content. I unglued myself from the window and drove to my office.

My coworkers greeted me warmly. I answered questions about maternity leave and proudly showed pictures of Max to anyone I talked to. Basically, I accomplished nothing at work other than reducing all of my colleagues' productivity. And I lasted only two hours before racing out of the office to snatch Max.

The next day, I lasted about three hours before running out of work to pick him up. By the end of a month, I was able to drop him off and focus on my work until it was time to pick him up.

I was enjoying taking care of Max and getting back into my career, both of which were balancing well. I found I had some bandwidth left over to do some more work on myself. My time with Janis was about maintaining the progress I made during my pregnancy and during Max's first months. My goal was that Max's environment, be it my womb or home, was calm, so I'd stopped pushing myself in my growth work. I had plateaued. I still had commitment and intimacy issues and wanted to put my foot on the gas at resolving those. And I still felt more comfortable when relationships were at surface level.

I now wanted to go beyond patching up emotional wounds and make the most of my precious time on this earth. And to be a role model for Max as someone who was thriving. My inner world was relatively centered and calm, and I was ready to take on more.

Janis was onboard and introduced me to the Internal Family Systems model (IFS). "There are multiple components within that are often in conflict. At times, a part of us feels one way, but another part of us feels another way."

This inner tug-of-war made sense to me. A part of me strove for independence, and another part of me wanted intimacy. It seemed a bit like the angel on your shoulder telling you to work out, while the devil on your other shoulder is telling you eat ice cream. I needed to figure out how to balance these warring parts to do both—to get some exercise and allow myself ice cream in moderation.

"IFS focuses on increasing your ability for self-leadership by understanding the parts of yourself and tapping into your core self." This didn't make sense until she guided me through an exercise.

Janis asked me to close my eyes and go inward. She then asked me how I was feeling about Max's nanny being late again.

"I feel frustrated. Angry, actually."

She told me to ask that angry part of me to step aside.

"Please step aside, angry part," I said to myself, almost laughing because it seemed so absurd.

"What does the anger look like?" Janis asked.

An image immediately came into my head: "A red, angry cartoon-looking face."

Whoa! Where did that come from?

"Now, what do you feel or see?"

"I'm frustrated. I don't like this angry face."

"Please ask the frustrated part to step aside."

The frustrated face, which was yellow and cartoony in my mind, took a couple steps to the side.

"Now what do you see or feel?" Janis asked.

"I feel curious." I paused. "Weird. I see an image of a cave. I'm walking in. I see a little girl's back."

"Go on."

"The little girl has turned around to face me. Her eyes are these scary, red laser-looking things." I was a bit freaked out.

"How old is she?" asked Janis.

"About nine."

"Can you talk to her?"

I visualized myself crouching down in front of her, and the redness left her eyes. She was just a kid, about the same age I was when my mom went to jail. The unresolved trauma had been hiding out here for thirty years!

Janis asked me to thank the angry and frustrated faces for protecting her and for stepping aside. She then asked me to comfort the girl. "In this exercise, you put images to your emotions, and the angry face served a role in protecting you since you were little. It's on your side."

"Why do you think you are angry when your nanny is late?" she asked.

The answer came to me easily after the IFS exercise. "Because it concerns me that someone who is unreliable has my son in their care. This terrifies me."

"Do you have any other concerns about your nanny?"

"None come to mind. Max lights up when he sees her. She has twenty years of experience, I found her through an agency and her background check is clean. All her references raved about her. But they did say that their only complaint was that she was sometimes late."

Getting curious helped me gain perspective and discharged the sensation of anger flaring up inside me. I could see how the anger was just looking out for Max's well-being and alerting me, and I appreciated that because this emotion kept me more aware of my needs and my boundaries for myself and Max. Once I recognized these unpleasant emotions, I could explore them and gain deeper insights. This helped me to understand I can harness emotions and determine how I wanted to respond. In the case of my nanny, I changed her start time to fifteen minutes earlier.

The IFS exercise also shined a light on some deep-seated anger with my mom that I needed to handle.

PART IV

*The most beautiful people we have known
are those who have known defeat, known
suffering, known struggle, known loss, and
have found their way out of the depths.*
—Dr. Elisabeth Kübler-Ross

39

On a hike near my house, grief and anger from a deep place inside of me dislodged. I hung with it as the tears and the gut-wrenching pain drained out. The waves of grief rolled through my body, and I rolled with it. Calmness and a deep peace were all that was left. The green leaves of the trees against the blue sky popped, and the world looked like it was in 3-D. Birds were trilling. *Was this an awakening?*

Layers of anger, worry, fear, and shame peeled off—what emerged was core energy. My source was light. This was an experience beyond my ability to put it into words. I'd had this source of power within me all along, propelling me through life. It was like finding the Holy Grail.

The weights I was holding inside, like resentment, seemed to totally dissolve. From that day on, I viscerally knew that everything would be okay. Not necessarily easy, but okay.

I was ready to talk to my mom about the hurt I was still carrying from childhood, and I was ready to forgive her and to forgive myself. And, I wanted to apologize to the other people I had hurt. *If only I could go back in time.* Start from where you are today, I reminded myself.

Today was Angela's birthday. Angela was the first woman I'd loved. I had lived with her for a few years in my early twenties. I hadn't spoken to her in over fifteen years.

I pushed myself out of my comfort zone and sent her a message.

I wrote: "Hi. I hope you and your family are doing well. I hope you have a great birthday. Anyway, I owe you a long overdue apology and a thank you. During our time together, I was a selfish asshole, and you were really wonderful. I've recently learned that I have PTSD, and I've had to work through unresolved childhood stuff. It's no excuse, and

I'm sorry it took me so long to apologize. Anyway, I'm wishing you and your family well. Best, Sara."

Angela replied within hours.

"It's lovely to hear from you. Thank you for the birthday wishes and for sharing that with me. No apology is necessary. I had my own issues and mistakes during that time as well. Funny, I texted you recently, your number must be different now, I only bring it up because in that message I expressed how much I had learned and grown from our time together. That you would always hold a fond place in my heart, and that I hoped your life was full of happiness. Anyway, we are all good here. Life has been turned upside down (by COVID-19), but in many ways it's even been a blessing. I'd love to chat sometime and catch up on life. All the best and thank you." She included her phone number.

Maybe I wasn't as much of a monster as I thought I was. When Angela and I caught up on the phone, the conversation flowed for almost an hour. I was ecstatic to hear about the great life she'd built with her partner and about how awesome her kids were. She said, "the days are long, but the years are short."

Next, I needed to talk to my mother.

Luckily, she spent a lot of time with Max, which allowed time for us to talk when he was napping. She opened the door to the conversation by telling me about a phone call she had with her aunt the night before. She told me that they'd spoken about everything that had happened in *her* childhood. And that after they'd talked, she'd had the worst nightmare and had woken up soaked in sweat.

My poor mom hasn't healed her own wounds.

She talked a bit more about her past, the words and stories pouring out of her mouth. I had heard most of these stories before, but not all of them.

I waited patiently as she continued to talk, allowing her to process her trauma, and thanked her for bravely sharing her painful childhood memories.

"Things have changed a lot," she said. "Back then it was taboo to talk about bad things."

I shared with her my truth and talked about the things that had been harmful to me and her role in that. She listened. I told her how I'd had a wake-up call and that for much of my life, I had been trying to outrun my fears rather than run toward love.

She didn't seem to totally register what I was saying or apologize, but she listened intently and surprised me with her response. "I had a feeling you were going to say this."

"What do I do now?"

"Stay awake," she said.

"Do you have any regrets?" I asked her.

She paused for a while, and then said, "No, they were all learning experiences."

A couple of days later, she brought up the conversation again and told me that she did have one regret. She regretted the ways she wasn't there for me and my brother. She said, "I was looking for love from men, when I had it all along, right at home, with you and your brother." She added, "I wish I had put you and your brother first when you were growing up. I'm sorry I didn't."

"You did the best you could at the time." I meant it. She'd had her own share of trauma in her childhood, details of which aren't mine to share, and it limited her capacity to be the parent she had wanted to be. What matters now is that I can stop the cycle of trauma with my son.

40

After many months without nightmares, I thought I was out of the woods until I had another one.

I was looking out the window of my house, except it wasn't my house. The house had a brick interior wall with windows that overlooked a grassy hill. A group of kids was playing there. The oldest boy in the group attacked the younger children with a knife. I looked away, too squeamish to watch.

I looked through the window again. I saw the bodies of the younger children. The oldest boy had killed them. I called the police. I was on hold for a long time. My mom and my baby were in the house, and there was a killer outside. I was afraid that he'd retaliate for me calling the police.

I told the police what had happened, and I hung up the phone. I turned to see the killer in my kitchen. He was attacking my mom. "My son!" I screamed to myself. I picked up his phone, which he had set on my kitchen counter, and threw it to buy time. I grabbed my son and ran down the stairs. He chased me, but I escaped. I looked around. There was civil unrest and trash in the streets.

I woke up disoriented and sweaty. The clock said it was almost three in the morning. I went to Max's room to check on him. He was sleeping peacefully in his crib. I walked to the kitchen and downed a glass of water. I changed into a dry shirt and went back to bed. The second part of this dream continued.

The world still had an apocalyptic look. I joined a group of people who were resisting, trying to change the state of the world. We were manufacturing supplies outside in a grassy area on a conveyer belt and discussing how we could help. I led the authorities to the scene of the murder, and they sent out a search party to find the killer. A faceless person from the crowd came to me and told me that the murderer had been found, and the world appeared peaceful again. "Come with me," the person said. I entered a room that had an audience sitting in chairs around the stage as if a play was about to start. They were all wise-looking people in red robes. One of them looked at me and said, "We were expecting you. The enlightened one is here." They pointed to the center seat and motioned for me to sit next to the enlightened one.

I woke up the next morning exhausted, but my body was wired. I scooped Max out of his crib, kissed him a few extra times, and went about my day. Fortunately, I happened to have a therapy session with Janis that day and told her about my dream.

Janis reiterated that apocalyptic nightmares are often associated with early childhood trauma, before a child has a fully developed brain or the vocabulary to make sense of their world. "The fact that you took action despite your fear and got your son to safety is powerful. You also played a leadership role in the resistance against the bad forces. This is a resolution dream, which is an indicator that you have integrated your trauma."

This was amazing news. From my understanding, integration was a key goal in trauma recovery, and as I read more about it, I learned that there was another step that some people took beyond that. It was referred to in different ways: post-traumatic growth, integration and meaning, or finding purpose. That is what I wanted.

41

My eyes began to more readily spot small acts of kindness and service all around me. The toddler who was sitting next to Max in a sandbox gave him his shovel. They shared the same bucket as they happily scooped sand into it. A woman held open a restaurant door for me when my hands were full. My neighbor brought over extra tomatoes from her garden. It blew my mind how many tiny acts of service were around me regularly. My heart grew, and I vowed to find ways to be of service to others.

I got the opportunity to be on the advisory committee for Seattle Public School's career and technical education (CTE) pathway, which provided courses, support, and experiences for high school students who wanted to explore careers in business, technology, and health care.

One day, I received a message from the head of the CTE program asking me if I would be interested in teaching an introduction to medical careers course.

"Yes!" I was interested.

I spoke with my supervisor, as teaching would be an addition to my day job, and she was generous with her support. Before I knew it, I had an interview, and I went through the steps to get my teaching credentials. A couple of months later, I got dressed up, and I was ready to teach. Sort of ready.

The principal and the other teachers gave me advice: "Be authentic. Care."

But I also needed to understand the basics. "Should the students call me Sara?"

"No. They will call you Ms. Church."

"Do I do roll call at the beginning of class? What do I wear?"

Some of my questions were just nerves, as I had been provided with the policies, the curriculum, and a mentor. I reviewed the available files about the students. Some had high grades but low test scores, while others had low grades and high test scores. What the data points told me was that neither grades nor test scores gave me a clear picture of the capabilities of the students. Even the student with the lowest GPA had unique strengths that stood out. They all had potential, of course.

I taught at a public high school with a diverse student body in a socioeconomically mixed neighborhood. I showed up to my first day, and sure enough, the class was in attendance and on time. There were eighteen lovely faces, some looking at me while the others looked at their cell phones. I mispronounced a couple of names during attendance and had a couple technology glitches, but, all in all, it went well.

My second class made me understand why some people love teaching. The students were more active. One student bravely debated the child-health module: "Why does this only cover things like life expectancy of children and leave out their experience growing up?" The student was making a great point by touching on quality of life, an important metric in health care.

Over time, I realized how passionate many of these kids were about the human experience and making a difference. When I was in high school, I was debating whether to eat in the cafeteria or drive to Taco Bell for lunch. When my students weren't sneaking glances at their mobile phones, many of them were discussing pursuing careers that contributed the most to society.

The students lit up my heart. I did my best to learn from them and to listen to get a better sense of their backstories. They came from various walks of life: A straight-A student who had immigrated from Central America and whose mother was very engaged with his learning. Another student who had grown up in the care of her grandmother and seemed a lot older than her years. And a student who came from a high-income home who wanted to be an artist.

It wasn't until the end of the first semester that it dawned on me that my personal experience with trauma was an asset. Dwayne, a sixteen-year-old boy who was in the foster care system, wanted to be a child psychologist to help kids. He was talented and had strong test scores, but his GPA wasn't great because he didn't turn in a lot of his assignments.

"Dwayne," I said to him one day, "I want you to be the group leader for the cardiology case." His eyes bulged. He stiffened. Had I triggered him? I let my question hang in the air, patiently waiting for him to answer.

In a rushed voice, he said, "Ms. Church, what's the point of doing this case? It won't help me become a child psychologist." I remembered that he had previously shared that he felt like he didn't fit in at school, and he had also written about racial inequities in the health care system for his last assignment. I am white, and Dwayne is Black, and I didn't know what it felt like to walk in his shoes or what about being group leader was bothering him, but I did know that my alarm bells were going off. Dwayne was having some sort of reaction to my request for him to be a group leader, which meant that it could have been a trigger.

The other students looked surprised and leaned forward as if I were going to send Dwayne to the principal's office for being defiant. I'd never sent a student to the principal's office. I took my time to respond. I wanted to make sure I was centered. "Thank you for bringing this up. It can take a lot of courage to ask questions like these." Dwayne's eyes were back to normal size. "Do you feel like this about this particular case study, or do you often feel like this in school?"

"In all my classes."

"I'll bet other students wonder the same thing at times." A few students nodded. "I had the same question in high school." I proceeded to give Dwayne an example of how the case could help him in his profession later in life. And I let them all know that I still used things I'd learned in high school, even though at that time I may not have known what the point of it was.

Dwayne accepted this, and he started turning in all his assignments on time. This was the first time I felt, at the heart level, that trauma had gifts to offer. Sure, I had convinced myself that adversity made me stronger, but I was rationalizing back then. I had spent so much energy trying to rip out my trauma from the root and eliminate it, leveraging therapy, meditation, exercise, neurofeedback, and journaling, that I didn't bother to appreciate the benefits. Frankly, I wasn't able to eliminate PTSD. The better approach was to transform it, and I was able to transform it into something else that could serve a better, positive purpose. While I don't see PTSD as my identity or a life sentence, my background is weaved into who I am.

I don't know which healing technique helped me the most; in a sense, they all contributed to getting me to this place. It is a beautiful place, where I feel fully alive and whole. There was a lot of trial and error, circles, steps backward, and steps forward. I fell and got up even when it seemed impossible.

As my mindset shifted toward service, I started with easy ways of contributing like holding the door open when someone had full hands, thanking each health care worker that helped my mom when she was in the hospital, or learning about access barriers for mental health care.

I got connected with the CPTSD Foundation, a community that I wished I had found at the beginning of my journey. The stories shared by these brave people spoke to me and made me understand the potency that storytelling has in healing. And it made me realize there is lack of awareness of mental health issues, in part because so many of us hide our struggles.

Thanks to the CPTSD Foundation, I found the courage to publish an article from my journal for the foundation's blog. My journal became the foundation for this book. Writing it helped me grow, and maybe, just maybe, my story will be able to help somebody else.

EPILOGUE

I have a desire to give you a Hollywood fairytale ending—maybe a wedding scene that takes place on a beach with my little boy in a tux holding a pillow with a ring on it—but that's not life, or at least, not my life. It wouldn't be authentic or accurate to package everything into a perfect box and tie a bow around it.

And I wish I could tell you I am cured and don't ever have any PTSD symptoms, but that would be a lie, and anyone claiming a quick fix is probably selling snake oil. The title of this book is "mending my mind" rather than "mended my mind" for that reason.

But I have made significant progress. My journey continues, and I am loving it. My inner world is generally peaceful and positive, and my life is much more joyful and fulfilling. The best way I have learned to honor my life is by listening to and living the truth in my heart. My future didn't turn out how I planned, but the stars needed to align how they did so I could have my beautiful son. I have what I always wanted, a family.

In writing this, I evaluated happiness and goodness and the many rigid social constructs and unrealistic messages we are bombarded with. I came to the seemingly obvious conclusion that it is absurd for me to try to fit in or to be perfect or happy all of the time. I'm human. I have done things I am proud of, and I have regrets. I still make mistakes and have a lot to learn. I have emotions that I enjoy and others I don't enjoy, but at least I am connected to myself. And I can still get triggered, which manifests as numbness or anger, but this happens a lot less frequently and I use tools to manage these challenges.

Also, I've installed practices, like daily walks and continuing with therapy as a safety net, to maintain the progress I've achieved and to further my growth. Although I don't see my therapist as often as I used to, I am grateful to her and the other experts that guided me through a challenging time.

Before Max goes to bed, we read a book, say a prayer, and list our gratitudes for the day. There is not a day that goes by that I don't have a solid list of beautiful moments. And I have a deep appreciation for how fortunate I am to have broad access to health care. While I made the choice to deal with my issues and do the hard work, it is not lost on me that I had the privilege to be treated by experts in trauma, which is a big reason I have gotten better. But there are huge gaps and disparities in access to mental health care, and this has negative consequences for individuals, families, and society. According to the National Alliance on Mental Illness (NAMI), "Nearly half of the 60 million adults and children living with mental health conditions in the United States go without any treatment."[1]

I believe healing ourselves will help us to collectively heal the problems in our world. And enjoy our lives more.

People I have opened up to, including my closest friends, about my complex PTSD diagnosis were surprised because I was able to put on a mask and hide it from others.

Struggle is universal. Most of us are personally touched by issues of mental health, and many of us remain quiet. I hope more of us remove any cloaks of shame we might be wearing by sharing our stories to just one person we trust. Together, through storytelling, we can support each other to reduce the stigma around mental health issues and create more advocacy to expand access to mental health care.

Thank you for reading my story.

---

1 National Alliance on Mental Illness, "The Doctor Is Out," 2017, nami.org/Support-Education/ Publications-Reports/Public-Policy-Reports/The-Doctor-is-Out.

Resources

Here are a few resources that were helpful to me or mentioned to me by experts. I defer to licensed health care providers for diagnosis and treatment of mental health-related conditions.

Also, because not everyone has a library card or extra cash in their pocket to purchase a book, a free PDF of my book is posted at sarachurch.org.

Organizations

CPTSD Foundation
  (cptsdfoundation.org)

Ergos Institute of Traumatic Experiencing
  (somaticexperiencing.com/home)

Insight Meditation Society
  (dharma.org)

International Society for Traumatic Stress Studies
  (istss.org/home)

The JED Foundation
  (jedfoundation.org)

The Minded Institute
  (themindedinstitute.com/yoga-trauma-and-ptsd)

National Alliance on Mental Illness
  (nami.org/About-Mental-Illness/Mental-Health-Conditions/
  Posttraumatic-Stress-Disorder)

Books

The Body Keeps the Score by Bessel van der Kolk

Brain Rules for Baby by John Medina

The Choice by Dr. Edith Eger

The Gift by Dr. Edith Eger

The Gifts of Imperfection by Brené Brown
(brenebrown.com/thegifts-hub/)

The Happiest Baby on the Block by Harvey Karp, MD

How to Talk So Kids Will Listen . . . And Listen So Kids Will Talk
by Adele Faber and Elaine Mazlish

It's Not You, It's What Happened to You by Christine Courtois

Trauma and Memory by Peter A. Levine

Trauma-Proofing Your Kids by Peter A. Levine

What Happened to You? by Bruce D. Perry, MD, PhD, and
Oprah Winfrey

More information and a free pdf of this book
is available on sarachurch.org/resources/.

Acknowledgments

A sincere thank-you for your expertise and contributions to this project: Sharon Heller, PhD, Salvatore Borriello, Lindsey Alexander, Chin-Sun Lee, Emily Mahon, Liz Schreiter, Sharon Bially, and Jen Doherty.

Key people who appear in this book also reviewed the manuscript. Please accept my heartfelt thanks—for that review and for teaching me these life lessons.

Mom, I am thankful I am your daughter and you are my mother. Thank you for your unconditional love and contributions to this project.

Elizabeth, I am eternally grateful for your courage, strength, love, and support.

Max, Mama loves you with all of her heart.

About the Author

Sara Church is a biotech executive and an advocate for mental health. At age forty, upon discovering that she was suffering from complex post-traumatic stress disorder (c-PTSD) due to unresolved childhood trauma, Sara embarked on a quest to understand and overcome the condition holding her back in her personal relationships so she could live a more fulfilling life. *Mending My Mind* began as a journal she kept during that process. She has also authored a children's book, *A Giraffe Named Monroe,* which is a fun tale about generosity and resilience. Today, Sara continues to transform her own c-PTSD into a force for love and strength. She enjoys spending time with her family, hiking, reading, and traveling.

Printed in Great Britain
by Amazon